GRAPHIC LIBRARY™

INVENTIONS AND DISCOVERY

THE WRIGHT BROTHERS AND THE AIRPLANE

by Xavier Niz

illustrated by Steve Erwin,
Keith Williams, and
Charles Barnett III

Consultant:
Darrell Collins, Historian
Wright Brothers National Memorial
Manteo, North Carolina

Capstone press®

Mankato, Minnesota

Graphic Library is published by Capstone Press,
151 Good Counsel Drive, P.O. Box 669, Mankato, Minnesota 56002.
www.capstonepress.com

Printed in the United States of America

1 2 3 4 5 6 12 11 10 09 08 07

Library of Congress Cataloging-in-Publication Data
Niz, Xavier.
The Wright brothers and the airplane / by Xavier Niz; illustrated by Steve Erwin, Keith Williams, and Charles Barnett III.
p. cm. —(Graphic library—inventions and discovery)
Summary: "In graphic novel format, tells the story of how Wilbur and Orville Wright developed, tested, and successfully flew the first powered airplane"—Provided by publisher.
Includes bibliographical references and index.
ISBN-13: 978-0-7368-6845-7 (hardcover)
ISBN-10: 0-7368-6845-3 (hardcover)
ISBN-13: 978-0-7368-7897-5 (softcover pbk.)
ISBN-10: 0-7368-7897-1 (softcover pbk.)
1. Wright, Orville, 1871–1948—Juvenile literature. 2. Wright, Wilbur, 1867–1912—Juvenile literature. 3. Aeronautics—United States—Biography—Juvenile literature. I. Erwin, Steve, ill. II. Williams, Keith, 1958 Feb. 24– III. Barnett, Charles, III, ill. IV. Title. V. Series.
TL540.W7N59 2007
629.130092'273—dc22
[B] 2006023376

Designers
Bob Lentz and Thomas Emery

Colorist
Melissa Kaercher

Editor
Christine Peterson

Editor's note: Direct quotations from primary sources are indicated by a yellow background.

Direct quotations appear on the following pages:
Page 10, quote by Wilbur Wright as published in *The Bishop's Boys: A Life of Wilbur and Orville Wright* by Tom D. Crouch (New York: W. W. Norton, 1989).
Page 13, quote by Wilbur Wright as documented in *The Wright Brothers: A Biography Authorized by Orville Wright* by Fred C. Kelly (New York: Harcourt, Brace, and Company, 1943).

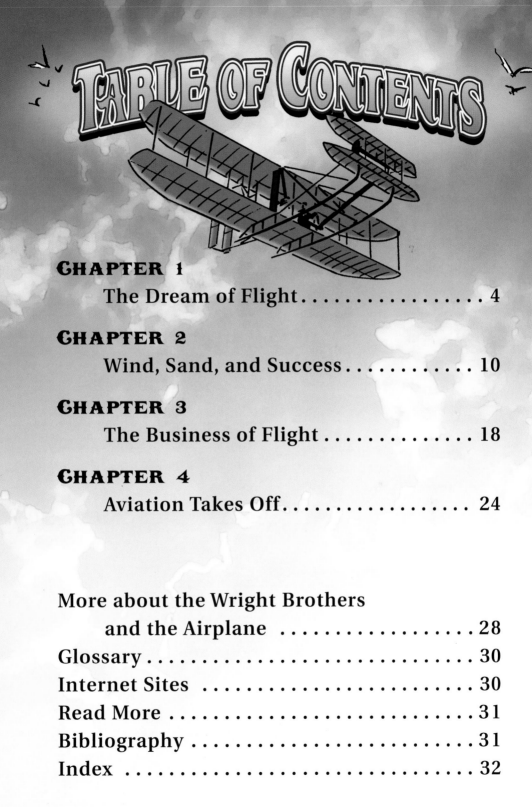

TABLE OF CONTENTS

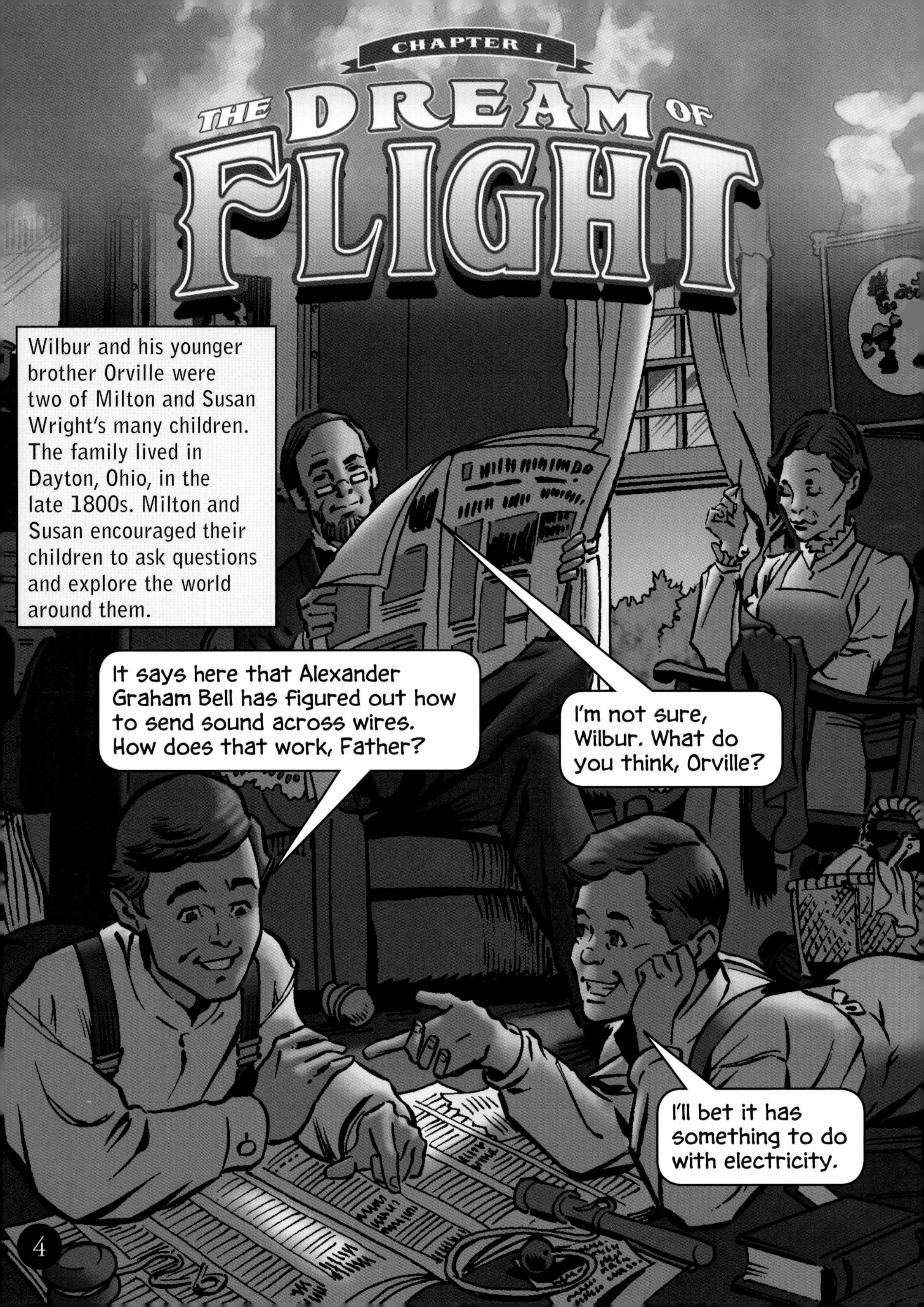
CHAPTER 1
THE DREAM OF FLIGHT
Wilbur and his younger brother Orville were two of Milton and Susan Wright's many children. The family lived in Dayton, Ohio, in the late 1800s. Milton and Susan encouraged their children to ask questions and explore the world around them.
It says here that Alexander Graham Bell has figured out how to send sound across wires. How does that work, Father?
I'm not sure, Wilbur. What do you think, Orville?
I'll bet it has something to do with electricity.

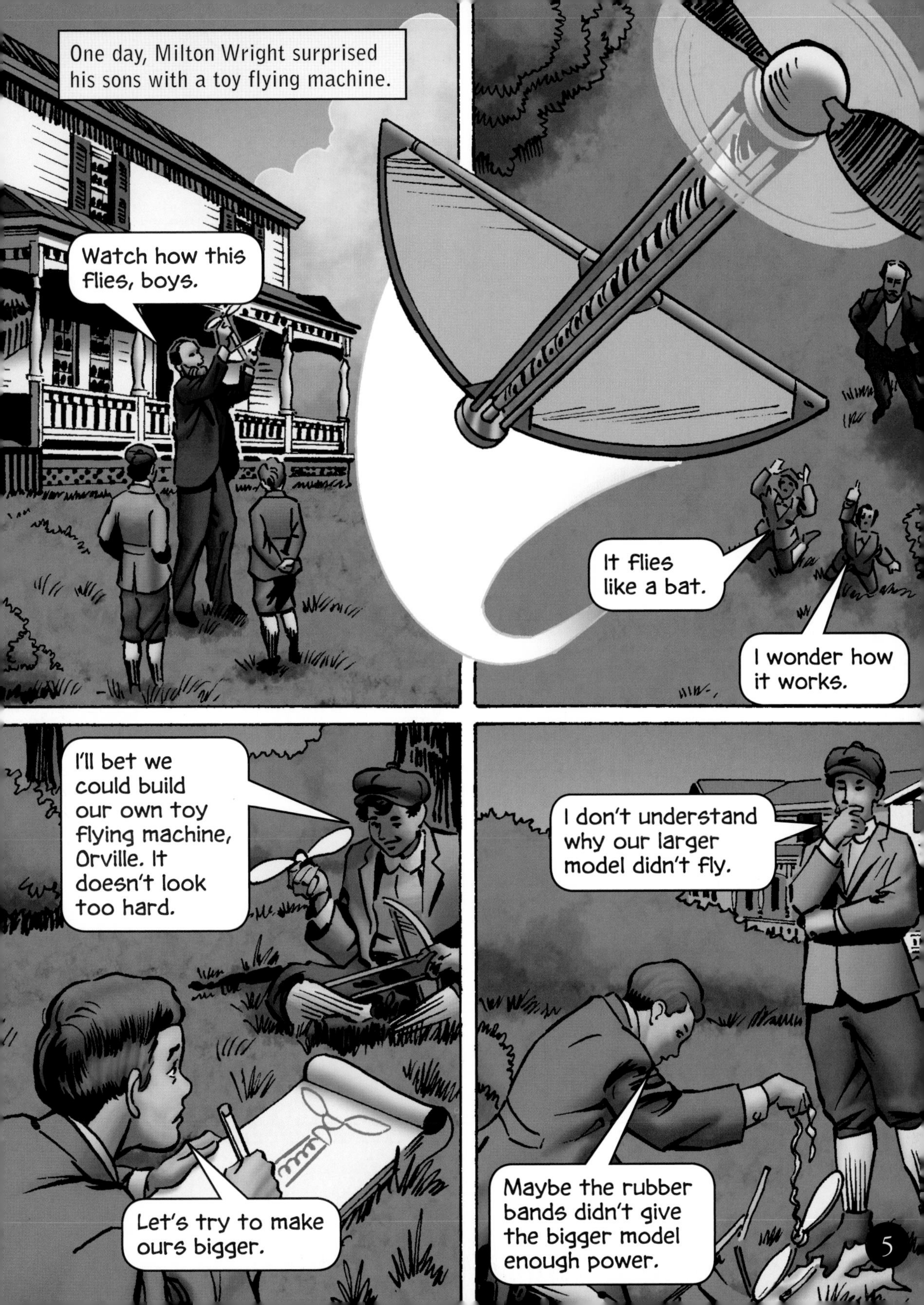

One day, Milton Wright surprised his sons with a toy flying machine.
Watch how this flies, boys.
It flies like a bat.
I wonder how it works.
I'll bet we could build our own toy flying machine, Orville. It doesn't look too hard.
Let's try to make ours bigger.
I don't understand why our larger model didn't fly.
Maybe the rubber bands didn't give the bigger model enough power.

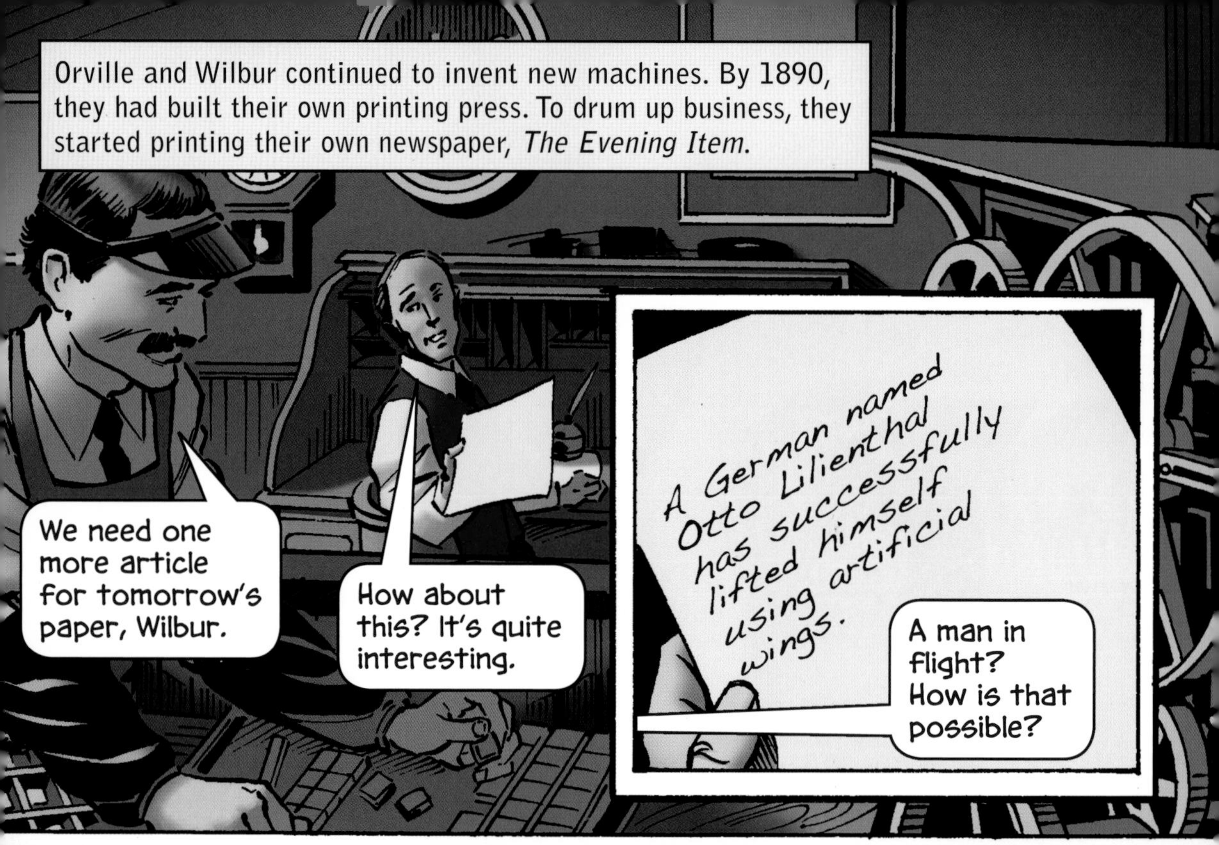
Orville and Wilbur continued to invent new machines. By 1890, they had built their own printing press. To drum up business, they started printing their own newspaper, *The Evening Item*.
We need one more article for tomorrow's paper, Wilbur.
How about this? It's quite interesting.
A German named Otto Lilienthal has successfully lifted himself using artificial wings.
A man in flight? How is that possible?

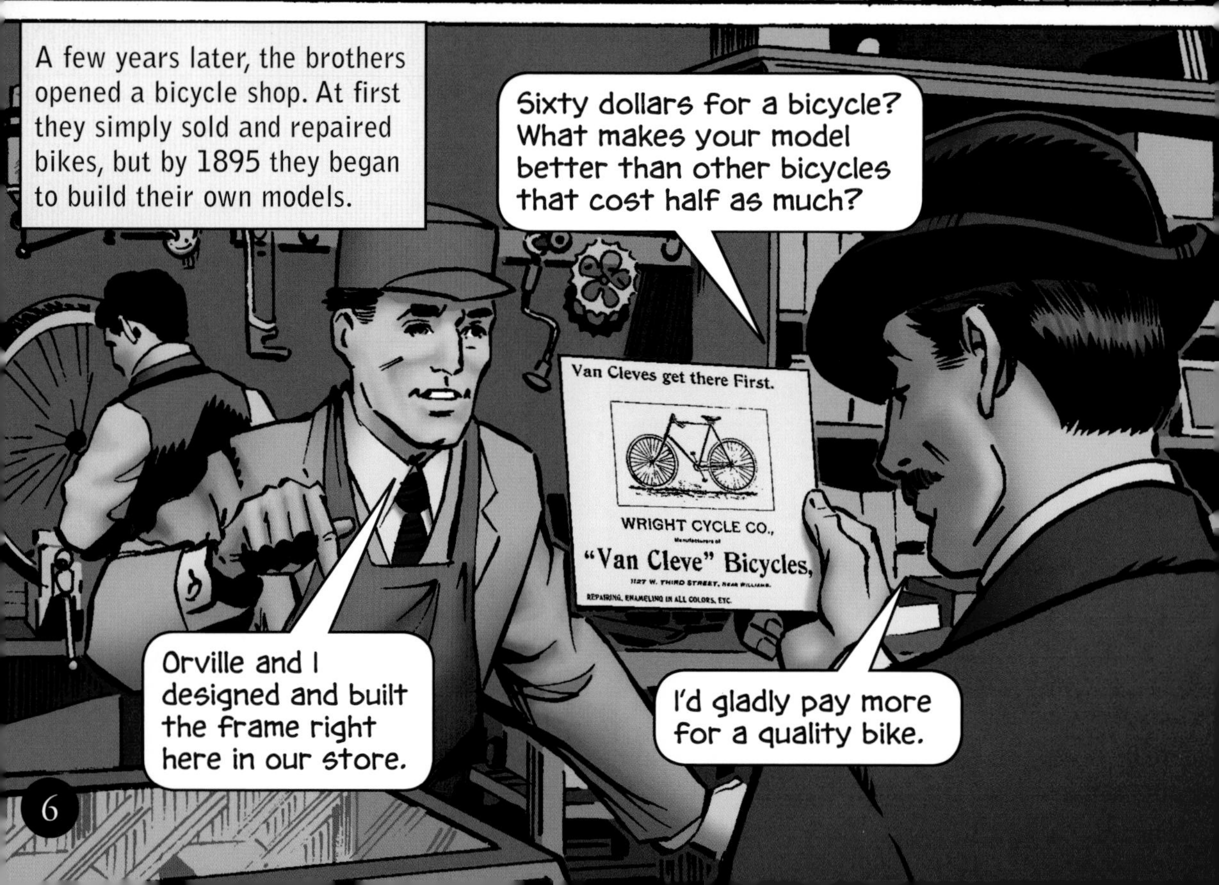
A few years later, the brothers opened a bicycle shop. At first they simply sold and repaired bikes, but by 1895 they began to build their own models.
Sixty dollars for a bicycle? What makes your model better than other bicycles that cost half as much?
Van Cleves get there First.
WRIGHT CYCLE CO.,
"Van Cleve" Bicycles,
REPAIRING, ENAMELING IN ALL COLORS, ETC.
Orville and I designed and built the frame right here in our store.
I'd gladly pay more for a quality bike.

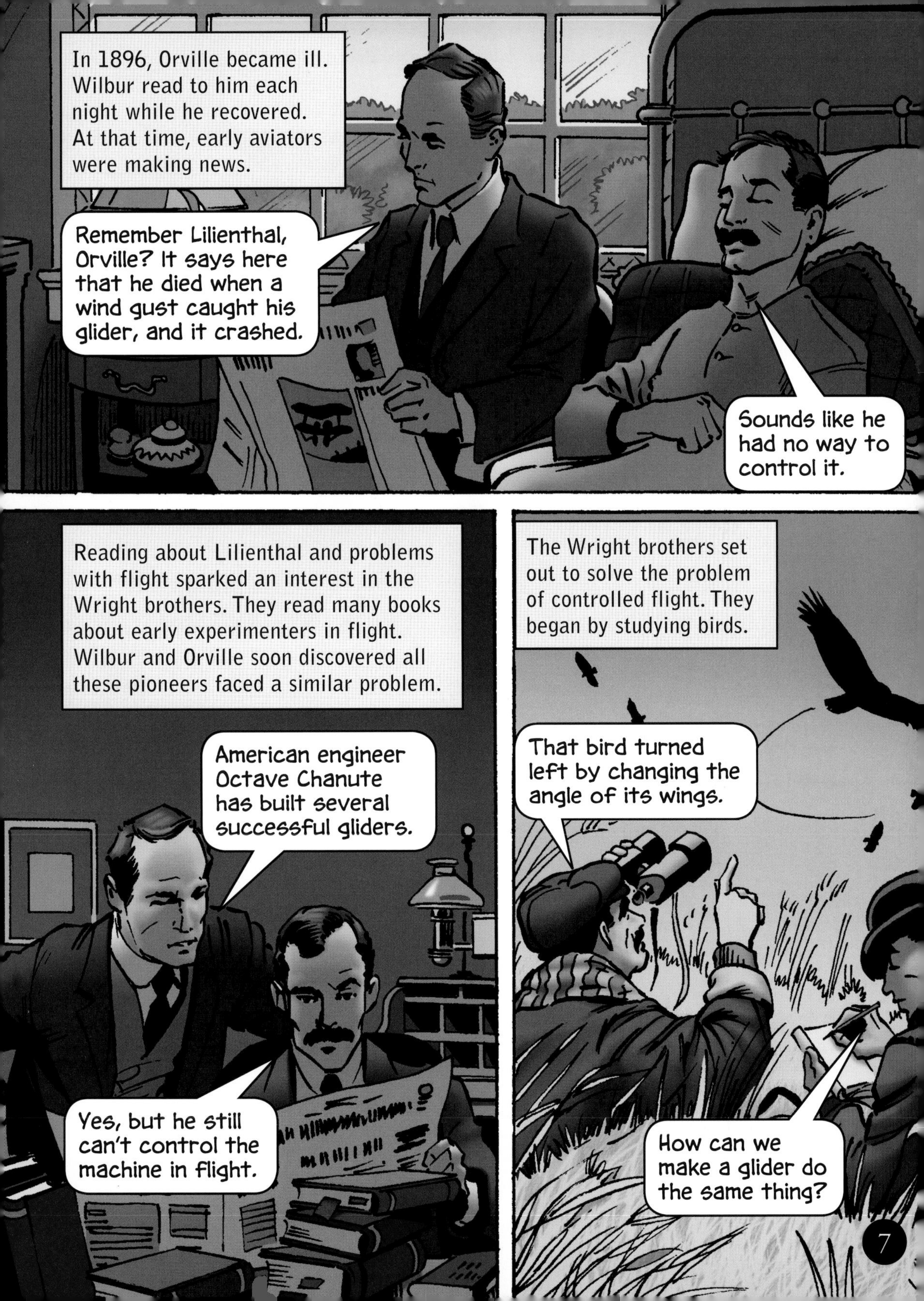
In 1896, Orville became ill. Wilbur read to him each night while he recovered. At that time, early aviators were making news.
Remember Lilienthal, Orville? It says here that he died when a wind gust caught his glider, and it crashed.
Sounds like he had no way to control it.
Reading about Lilienthal and problems with flight sparked an interest in the Wright brothers. They read many books about early experimenters in flight. Wilbur and Orville soon discovered all these pioneers faced a similar problem.
American engineer Octave Chanute has built several successful gliders.
Yes, but he still can't control the machine in flight.
The Wright brothers set out to solve the problem of controlled flight. They began by studying birds.
That bird turned left by changing the angle of its wings.
How can we make a glider do the same thing?

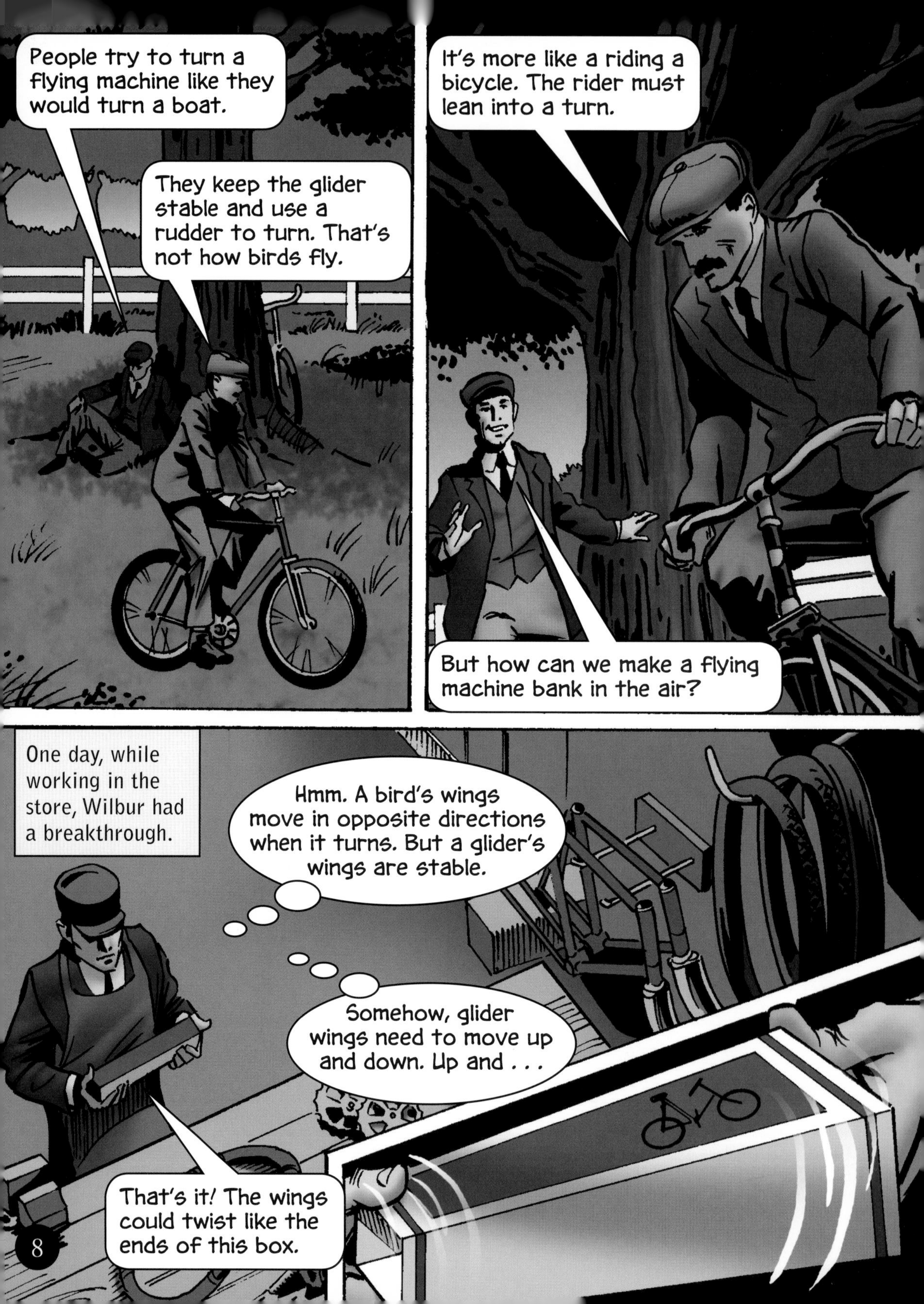
People try to turn a flying machine like they would turn a boat.
They keep the glider stable and use a rudder to turn. That's not how birds fly.
It's more like a riding a bicycle. The rider must lean into a turn.
But how can we make a flying machine bank in the air?
One day, while working in the store, Wilbur had a breakthrough.
Hmm. A bird's wings move in opposite directions when it turns. But a glider's wings are stable.
Somehow, glider wings need to move up and down. Up and . . .
That's it! The wings could twist like the ends of this box.

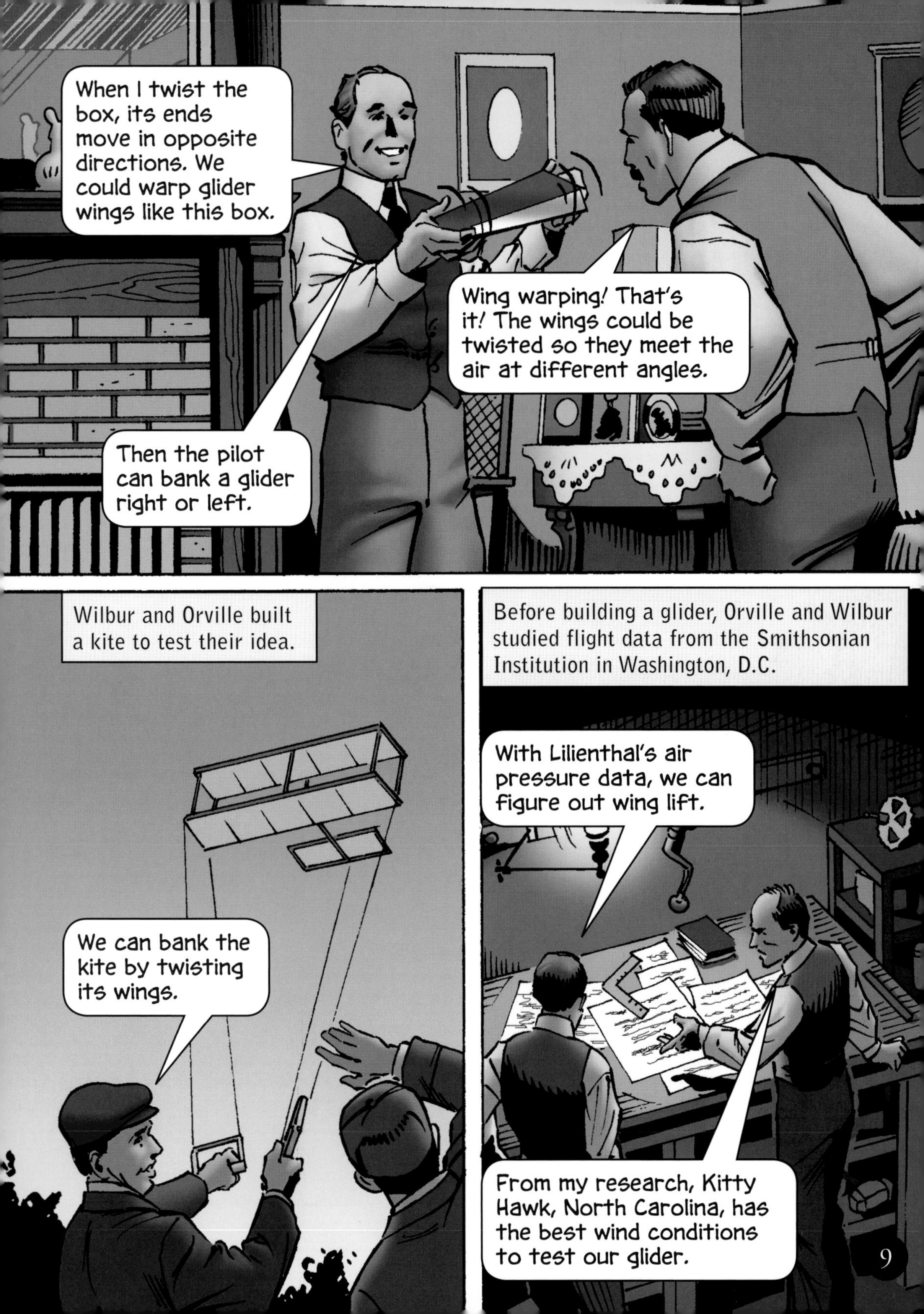
When I twist the box, its ends move in opposite directions. We could warp glider wings like this box.
Wing warping! That's it! The wings could be twisted so they meet the air at different angles.
Then the pilot can bank a glider right or left.
Wilbur and Orville built a kite to test their idea.
We can bank the kite by twisting its wings.
Before building a glider, Orville and Wilbur studied flight data from the Smithsonian Institution in Washington, D.C.
With Lilienthal's air pressure data, we can figure out wing lift.
From my research, Kitty Hawk, North Carolina, has the best wind conditions to test our glider.

CHAPTER 2

WIND, SAND AND SUCCESS

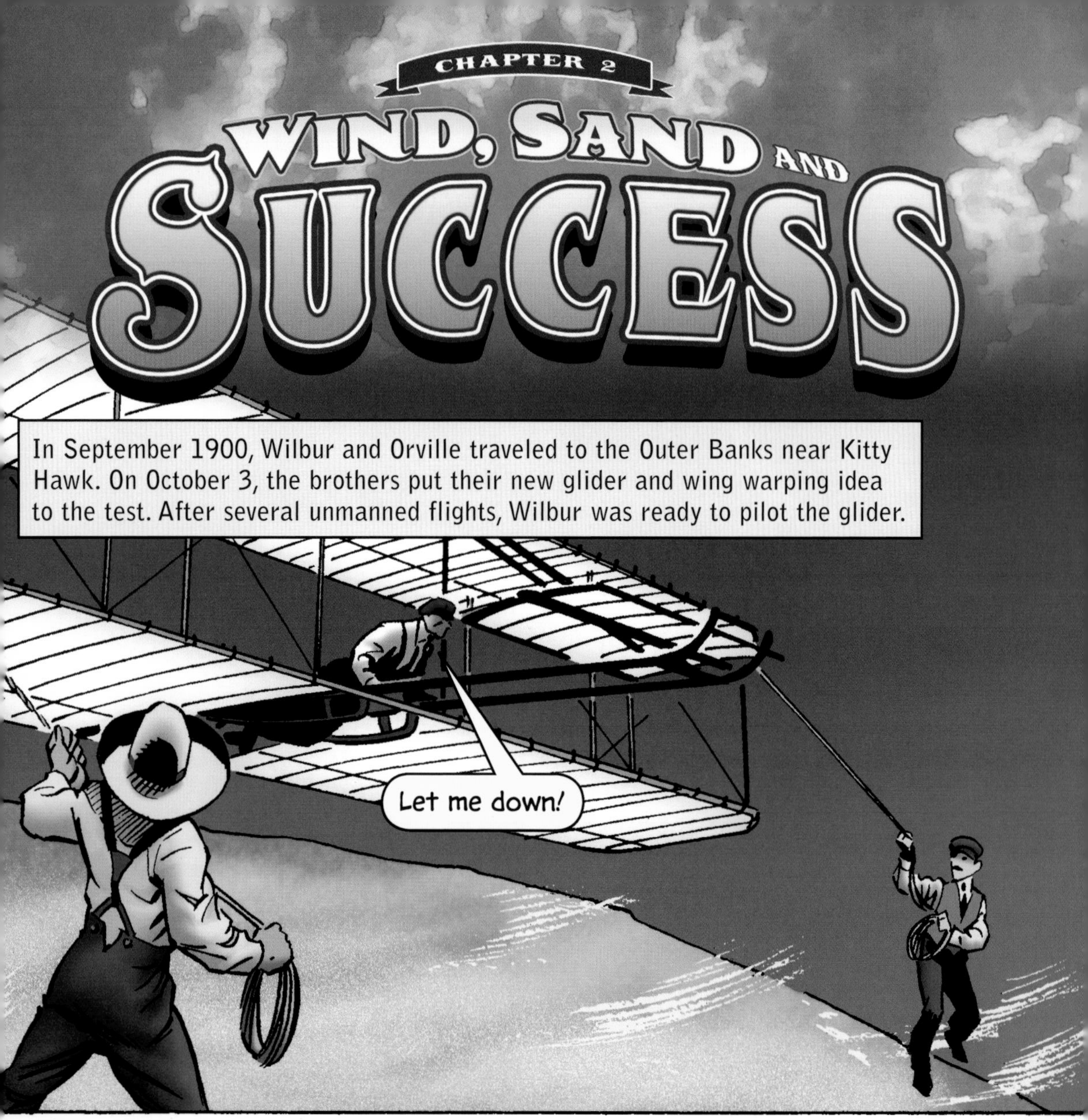
In September 1900, Wilbur and Orville traveled to the Outer Banks near Kitty Hawk. On October 3, the brothers put their new glider and wing warping idea to the test. After several unmanned flights, Wilbur was ready to pilot the glider.
Let me down!

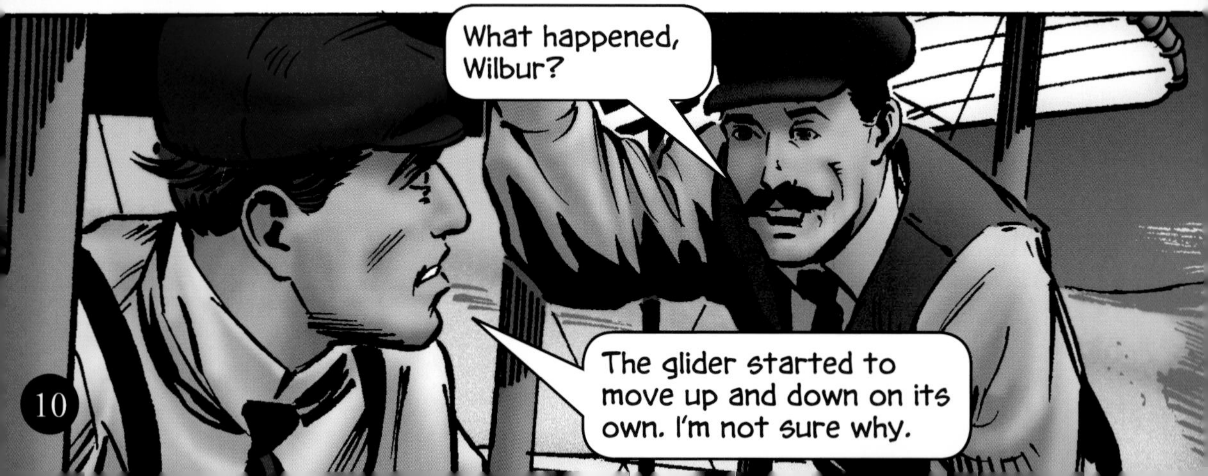
What happened, Wilbur?
The glider started to move up and down on its own. I'm not sure why.

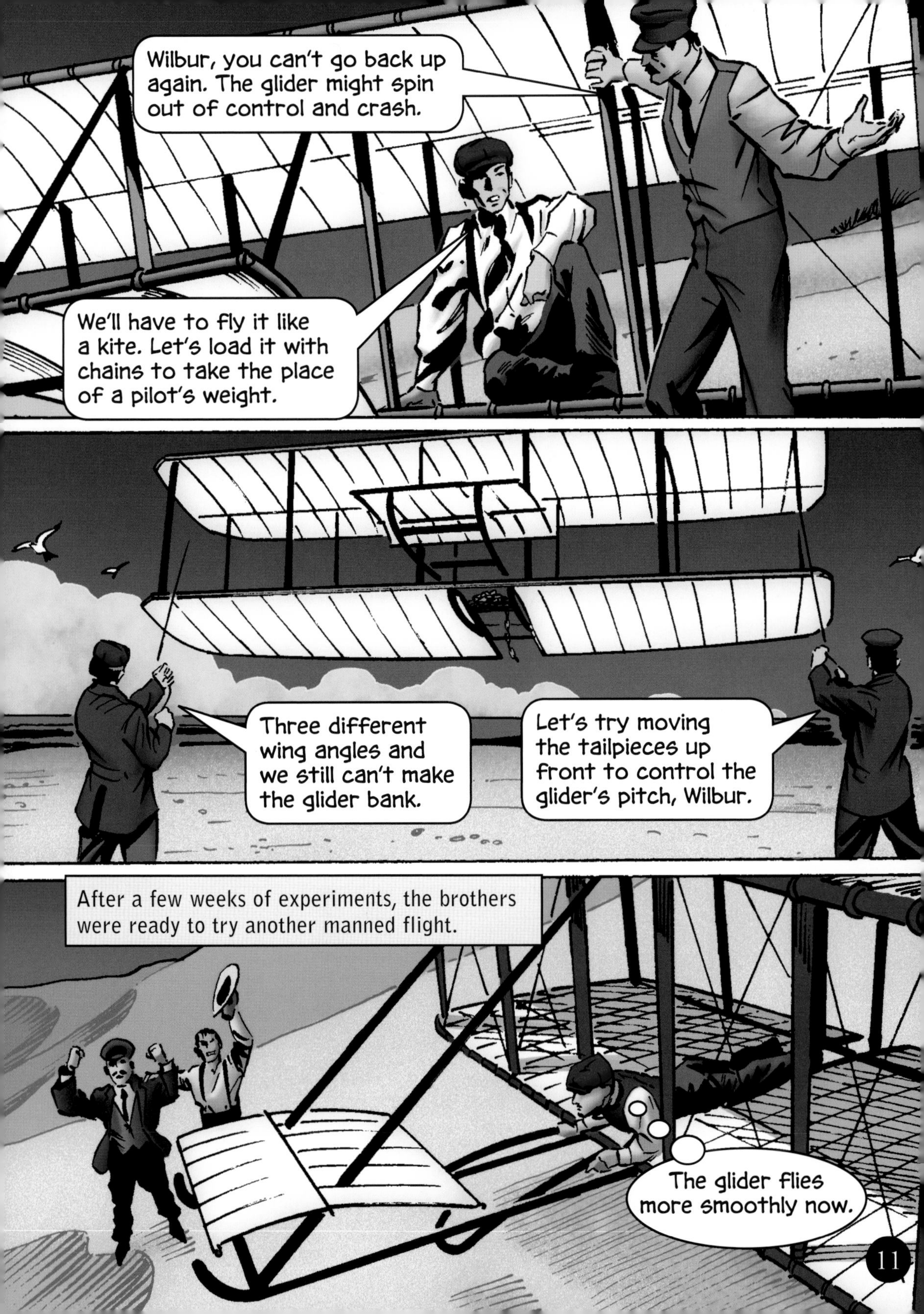
Wilbur, you can't go back up again. The glider might spin out of control and crash.
We'll have to fly it like a kite. Let's load it with chains to take the place of a pilot's weight.
Three different wing angles and we still can't make the glider bank.
Let's try moving the tailpieces up front to control the glider's pitch, Wilbur.
After a few weeks of experiments, the brothers were ready to try another manned flight.
The glider flies more smoothly now.

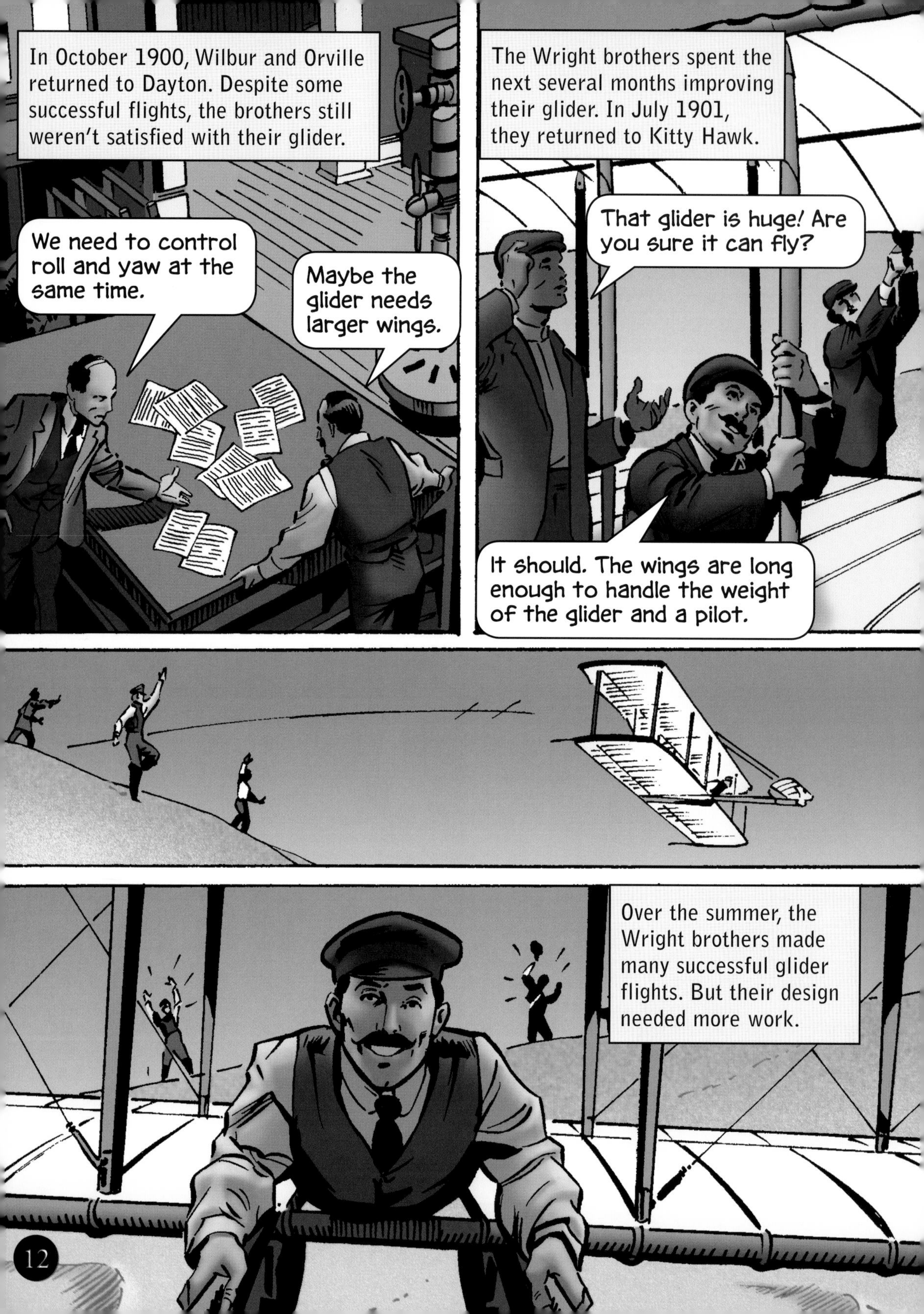
In October 1900, Wilbur and Orville returned to Dayton. Despite some successful flights, the brothers still weren't satisfied with their glider.
We need to control roll and yaw at the same time.
Maybe the glider needs larger wings.
The Wright brothers spent the next several months improving their glider. In July 1901, they returned to Kitty Hawk.
That glider is huge! Are you sure it can fly?
It should. The wings are long enough to handle the weight of the glider and a pilot.
Over the summer, the Wright brothers made many successful glider flights. But their design needed more work.

We'll need more lift for powered flight.

Perhaps there's something wrong with Lilienthal's data?

I'm beginning to think that not within a thousand years would man ever fly!

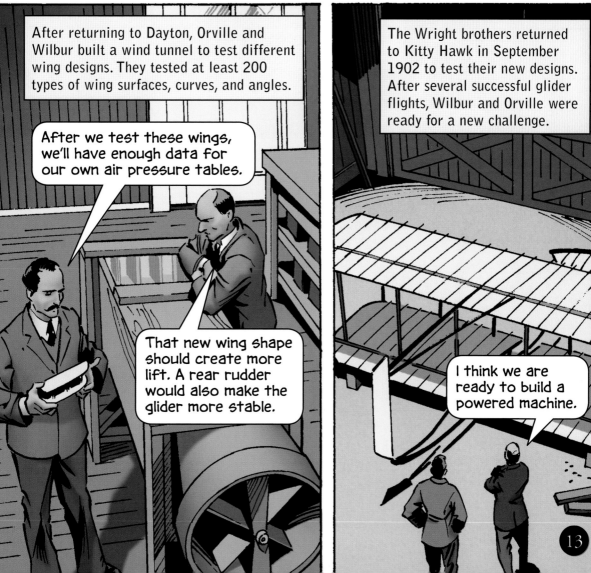

After returning to Dayton, Orville and Wilbur built a wind tunnel to test different wing designs. They tested at least 200 types of wing surfaces, curves, and angles.

After we test these wings, we'll have enough data for our own air pressure tables.

That new wing shape should create more lift. A rear rudder would also make the glider more stable.

The Wright brothers returned to Kitty Hawk in September 1902 to test their new designs. After several successful glider flights, Wilbur and Orville were ready for a new challenge.

I think we are ready to build a powered machine.

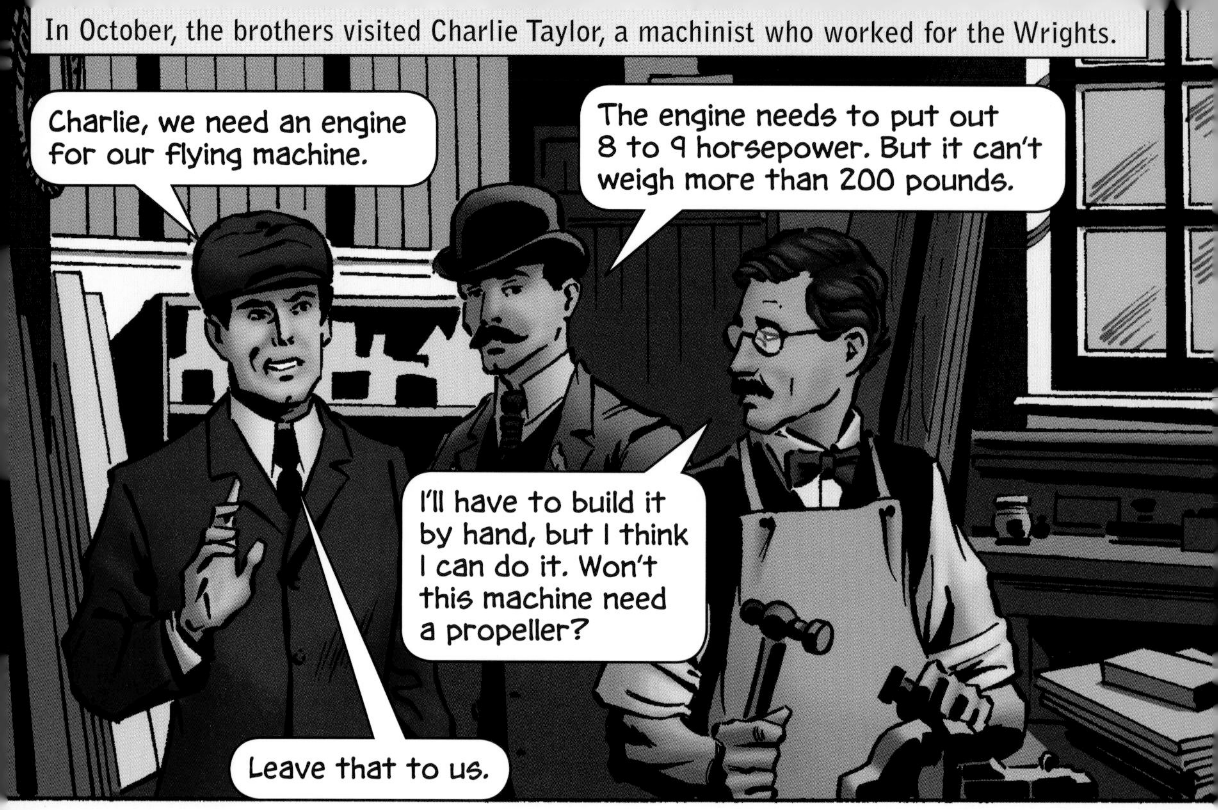
In October, the brothers visited Charlie Taylor, a machinist who worked for the Wrights.
Charlie, we need an engine for our flying machine.
The engine needs to put out 8 to 9 horsepower. But it can't weigh more than 200 pounds.
I'll have to build it by hand, but I think I can do it. Won't this machine need a propeller?
Leave that to us.

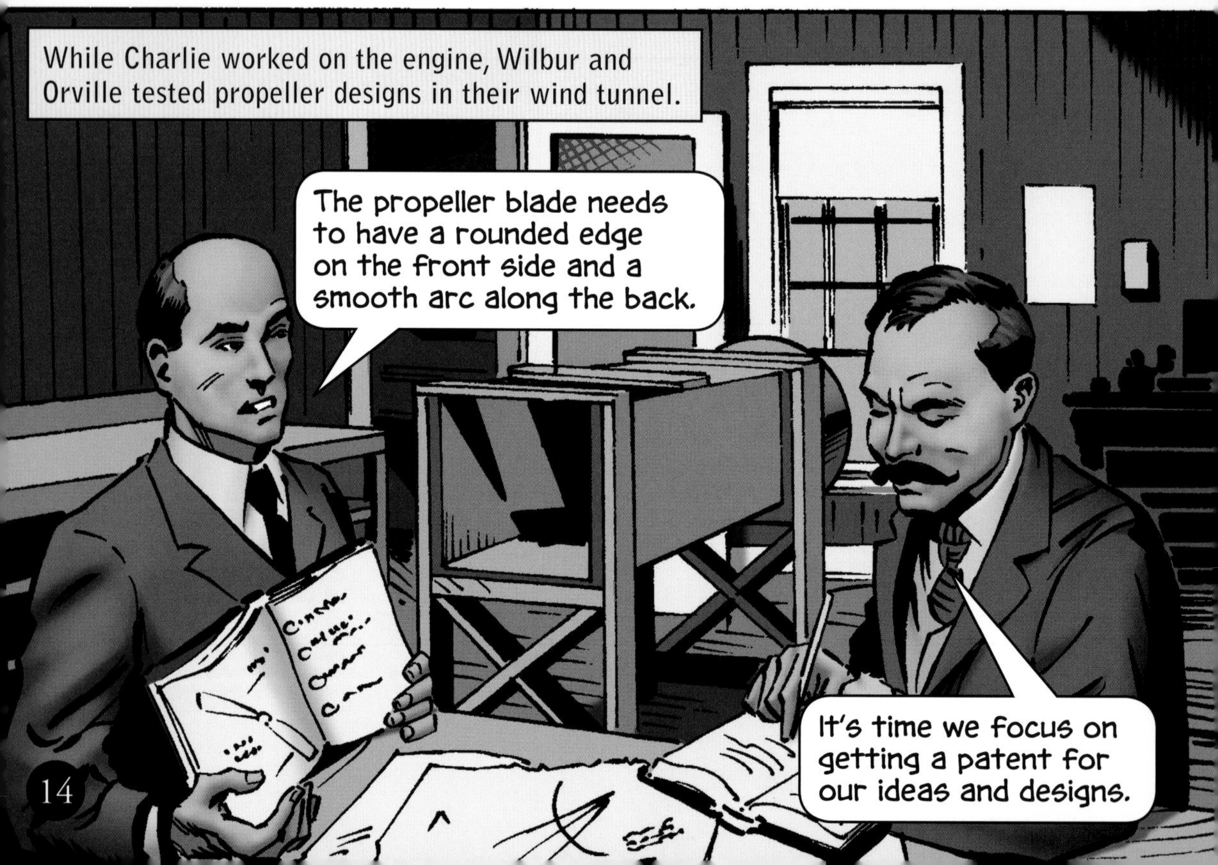
While Charlie worked on the engine, Wilbur and Orville tested propeller designs in their wind tunnel.
The propeller blade needs to have a rounded edge on the front side and a smooth arc along the back.
It's time we focus on getting a patent for our ideas and designs.

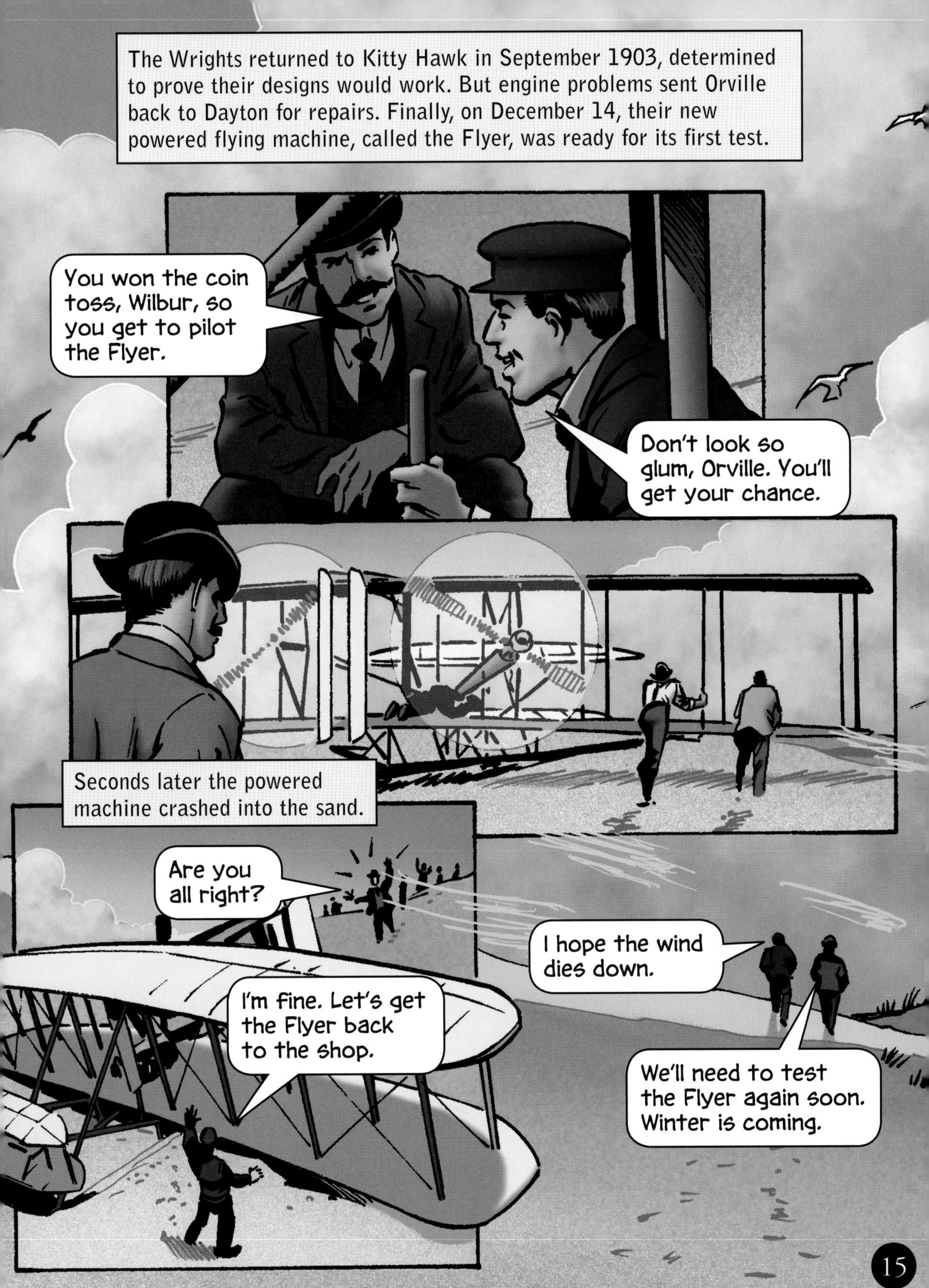
The Wrights returned to Kitty Hawk in September 1903, determined to prove their designs would work. But engine problems sent Orville back to Dayton for repairs. Finally, on December 14, their new powered flying machine, called the Flyer, was ready for its first test.
You won the coin toss, Wilbur, so you get to pilot the Flyer.
Don't look so glum, Orville. You'll get your chance.
Seconds later the powered machine crashed into the sand.
Are you all right?
I'm fine. Let's get the Flyer back to the shop.
I hope the wind dies down.
We'll need to test the Flyer again soon. Winter is coming.

On December 17, 1903, Orville and Wilbur decided to try one last flight. By 10:30 that morning, the Wrights and their crew had the Flyer positioned on its wooden launching rail.

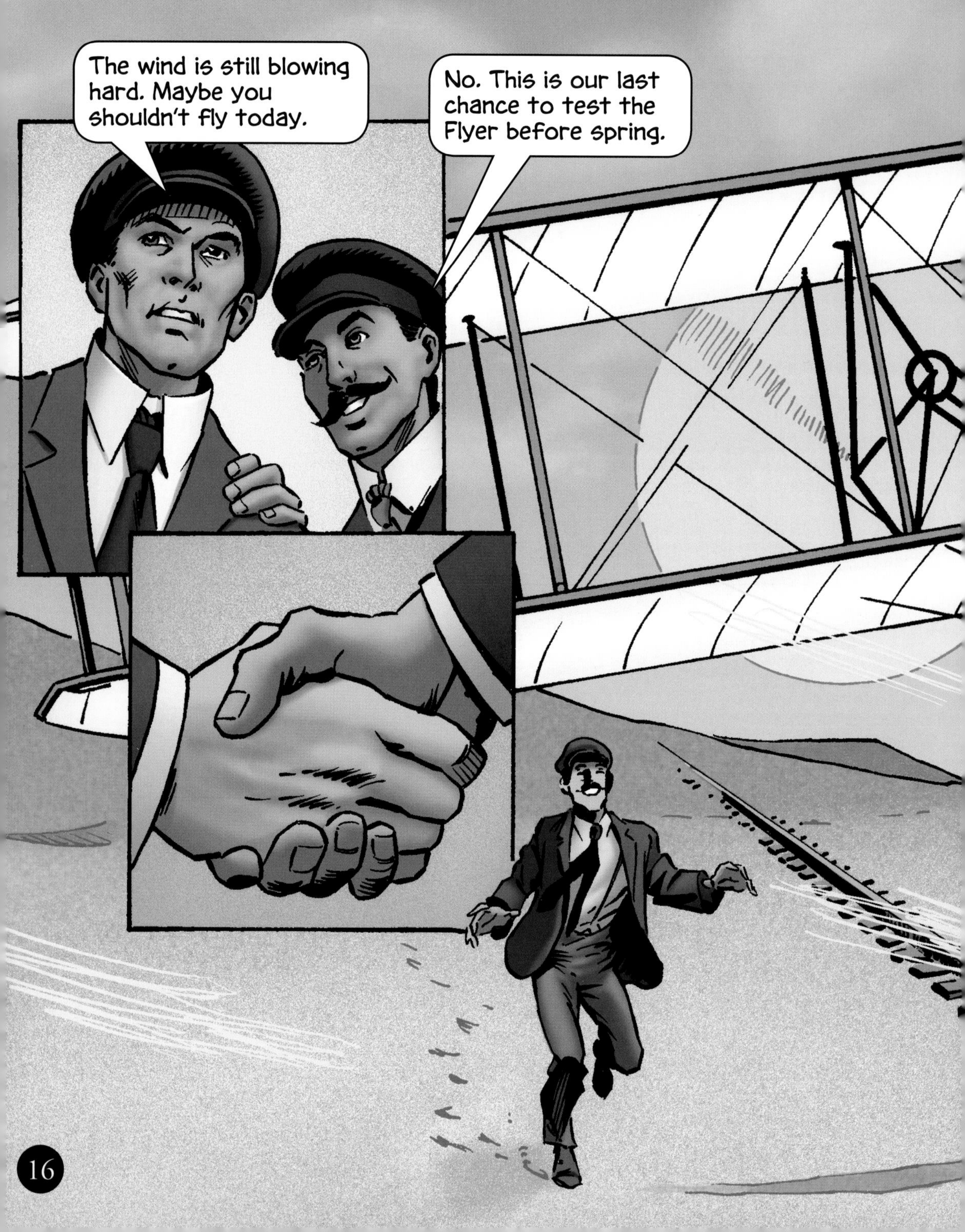
The wind is still blowing hard. Maybe you shouldn't fly today.
No. This is our last chance to test the Flyer before spring.

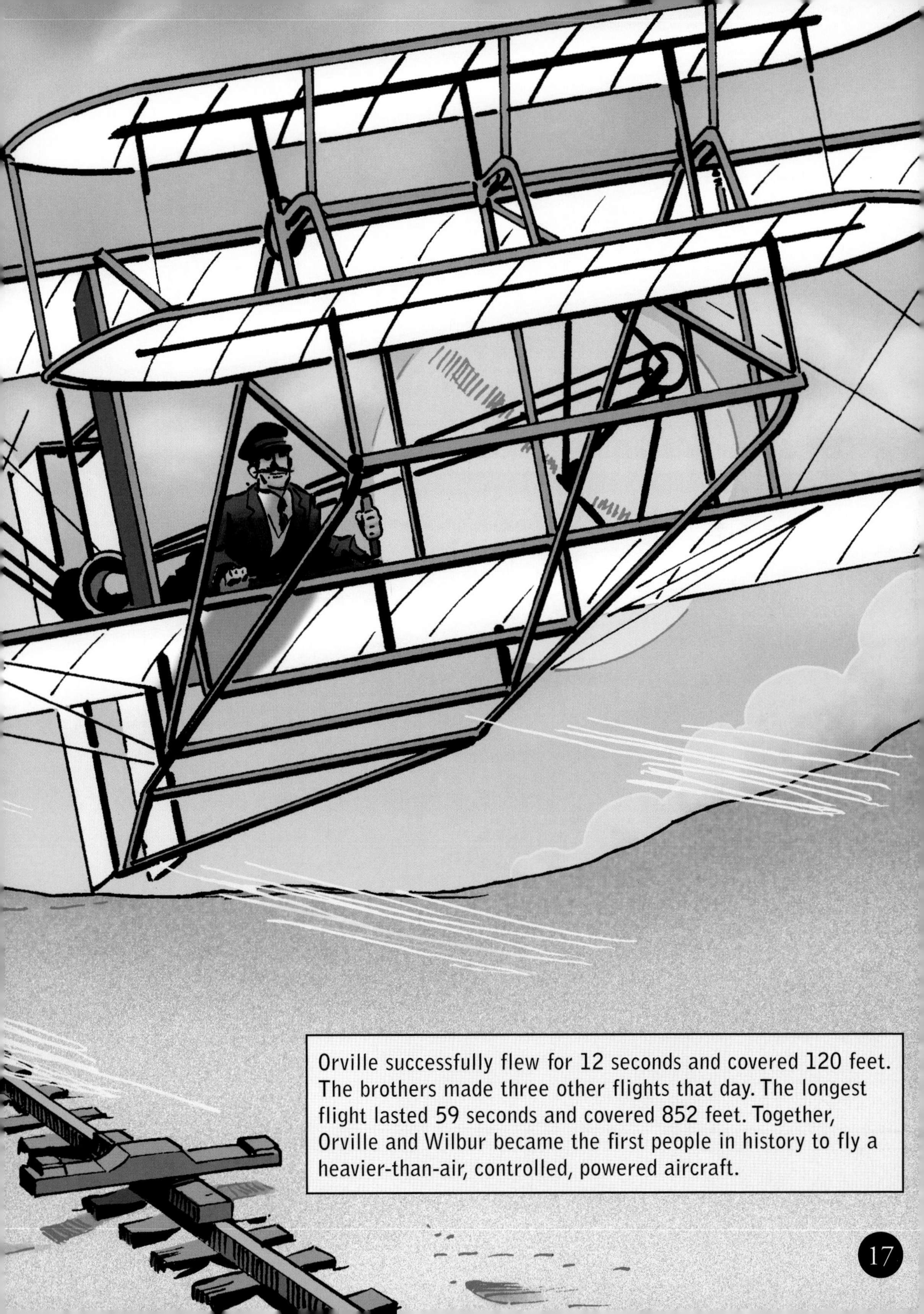
Orville successfully flew for 12 seconds and covered 120 feet. The brothers made three other flights that day. The longest flight lasted 59 seconds and covered 852 feet. Together, Orville and Wilbur became the first people in history to fly a heavier-than-air, controlled, powered aircraft.

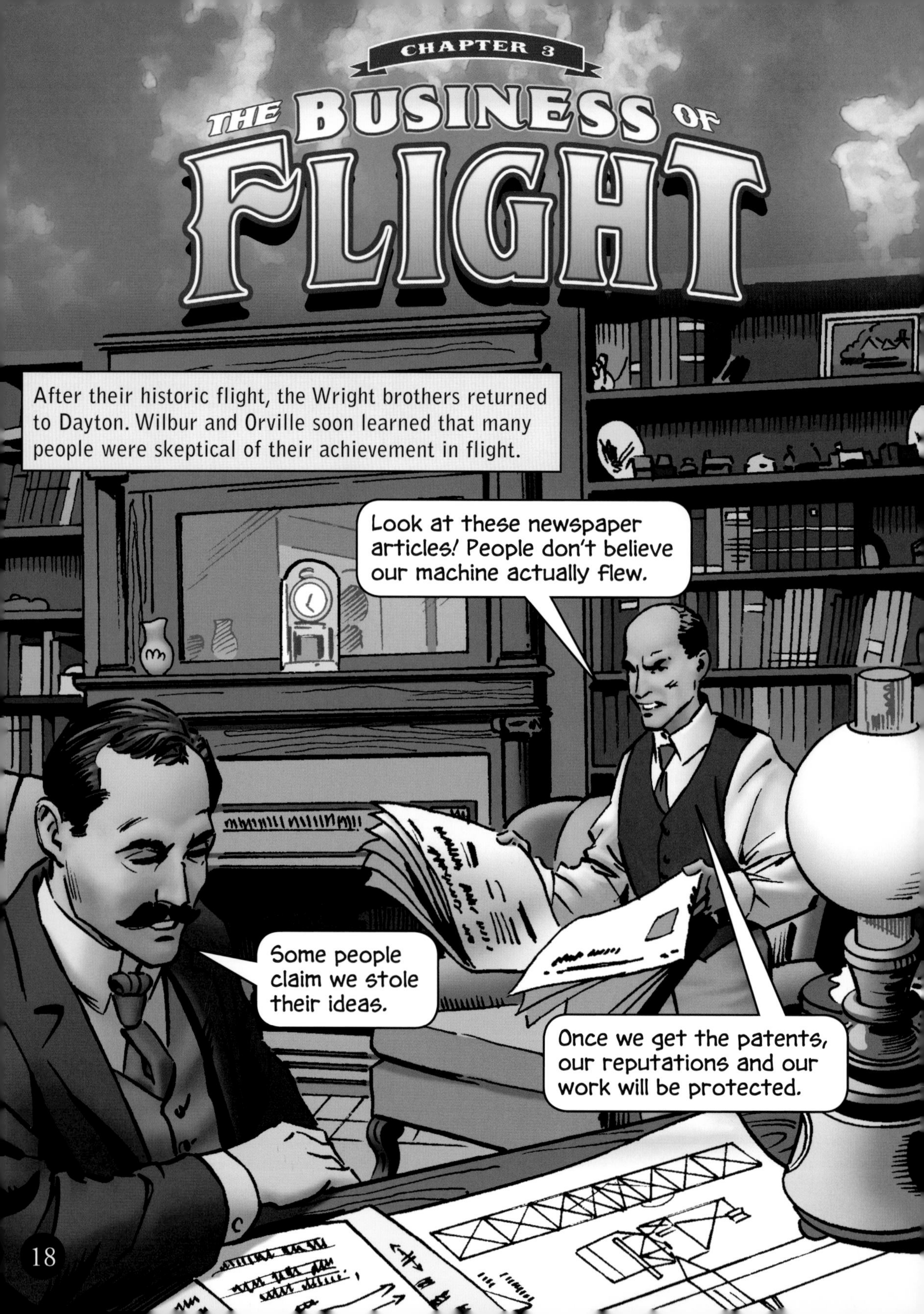
CHAPTER 3
THE BUSINESS OF FLIGHT
After their historic flight, the Wright brothers returned to Dayton. Wilbur and Orville soon learned that many people were skeptical of their achievement in flight.
Look at these newspaper articles! People don't believe our machine actually flew.
Some people claim we stole their ideas.
Once we get the patents, our reputations and our work will be protected.

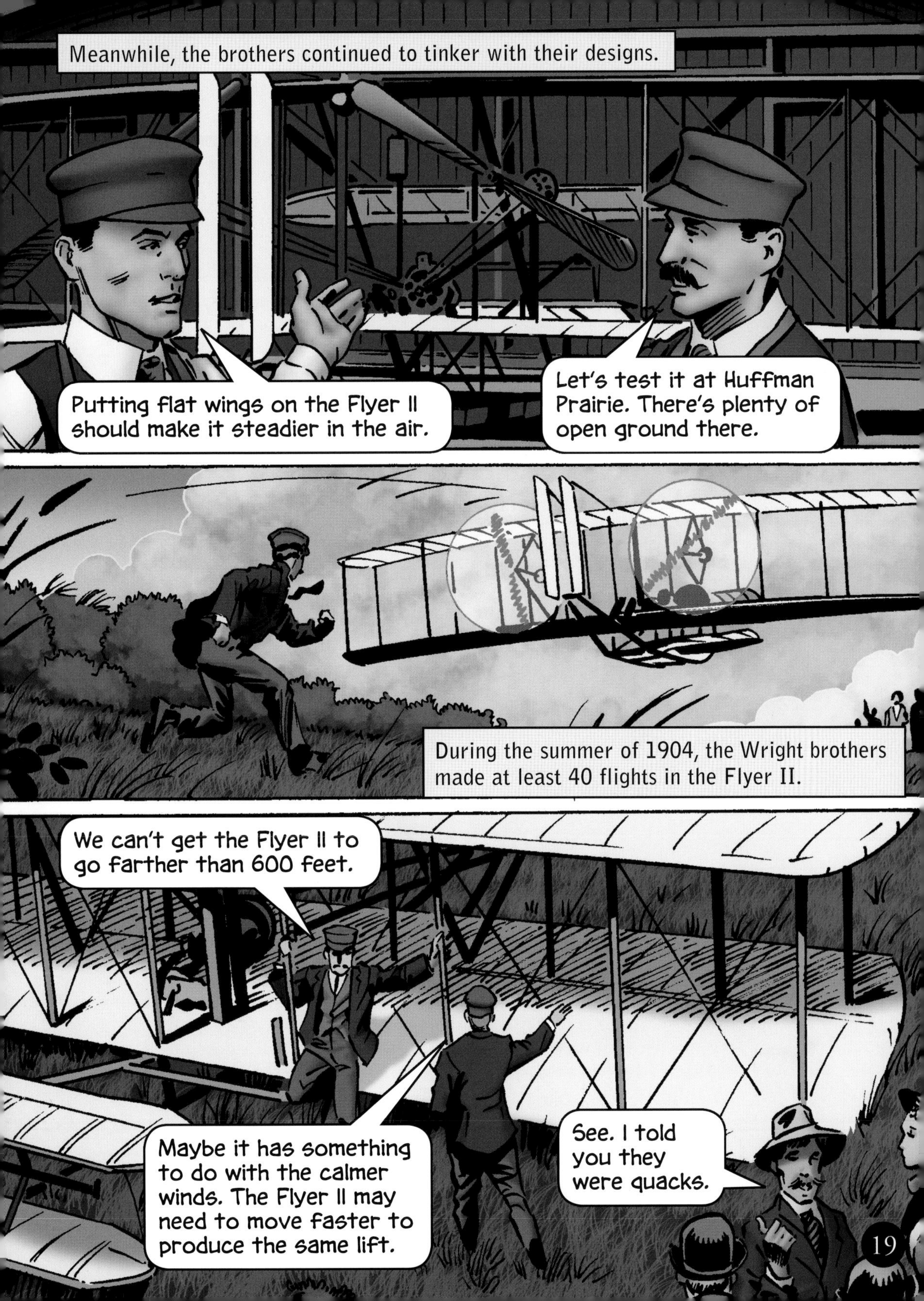
Meanwhile, the brothers continued to tinker with their designs.
Putting flat wings on the Flyer II should make it steadier in the air.
Let's test it at Huffman Prairie. There's plenty of open ground there.
During the summer of 1904, the Wright brothers made at least 40 flights in the Flyer II.
We can't get the Flyer II to go farther than 600 feet.
Maybe it has something to do with the calmer winds. The Flyer II may need to move faster to produce the same lift.
See. I told you they were quacks.

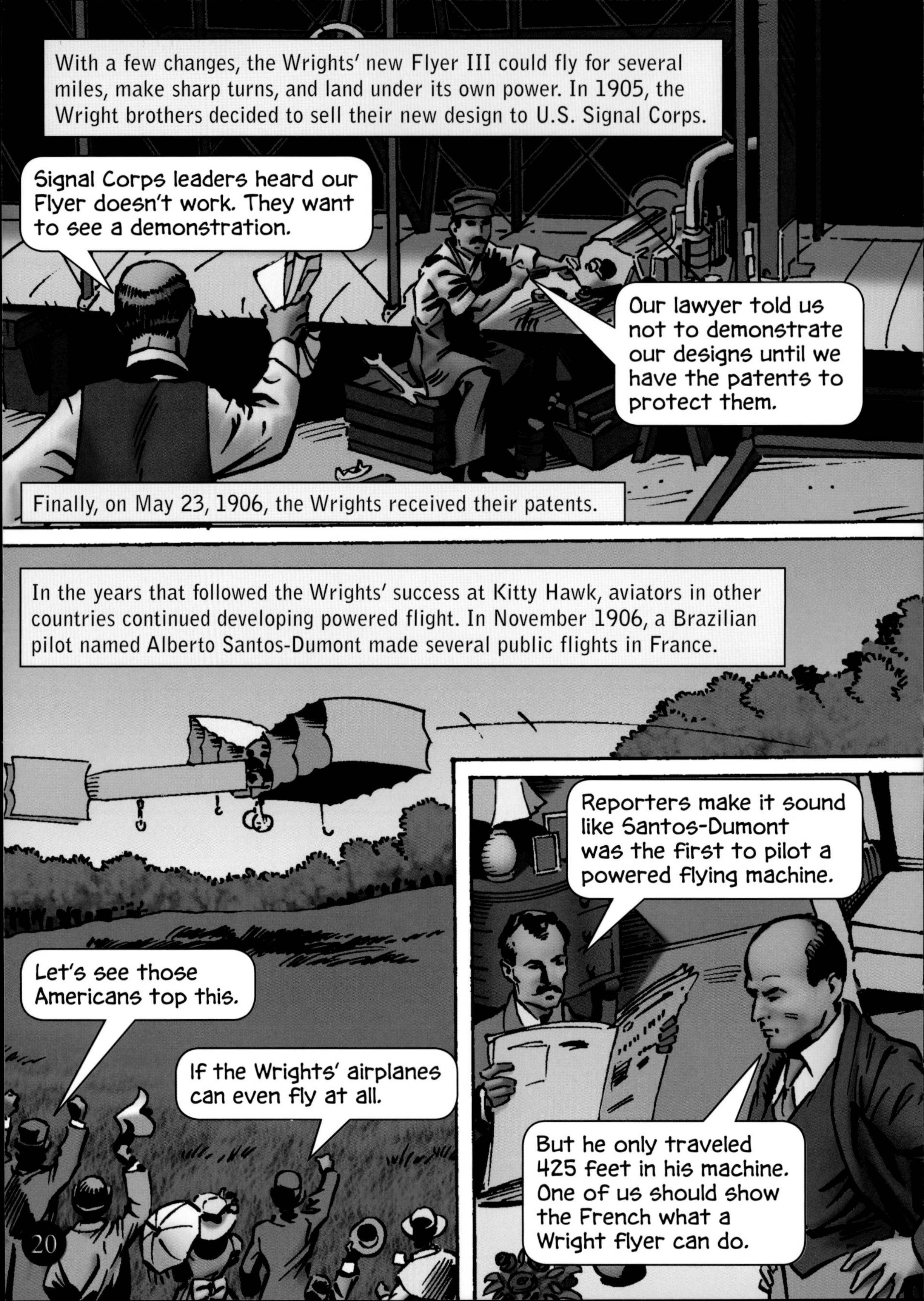
With a few changes, the Wrights' new Flyer III could fly for several miles, make sharp turns, and land under its own power. In 1905, the Wright brothers decided to sell their new design to U.S. Signal Corps.
Signal Corps leaders heard our Flyer doesn't work. They want to see a demonstration.
Our lawyer told us not to demonstrate our designs until we have the patents to protect them.
Finally, on May 23, 1906, the Wrights received their patents.
In the years that followed the Wrights' success at Kitty Hawk, aviators in other countries continued developing powered flight. In November 1906, a Brazilian pilot named Alberto Santos-Dumont made several public flights in France.
Let's see those Americans top this.
If the Wrights' airplanes can even fly at all.
Reporters make it sound like Santos-Dumont was the first to pilot a powered flying machine.
But he only traveled 425 feet in his machine. One of us should show the French what a Wright flyer can do.

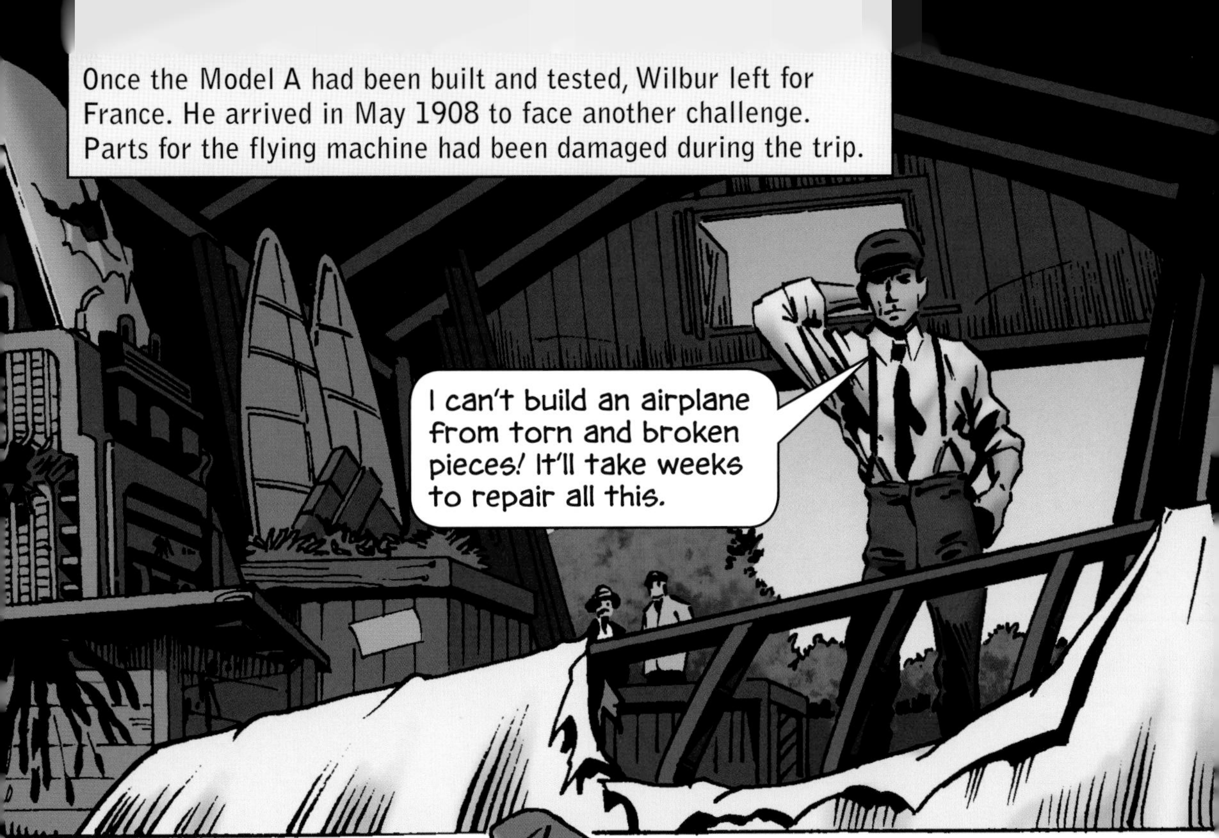
Once the Model A had been built and tested, Wilbur left for France. He arrived in May 1908 to face another challenge. Parts for the flying machine had been damaged during the trip.
I can't build an airplane from torn and broken pieces! It'll take weeks to repair all this.

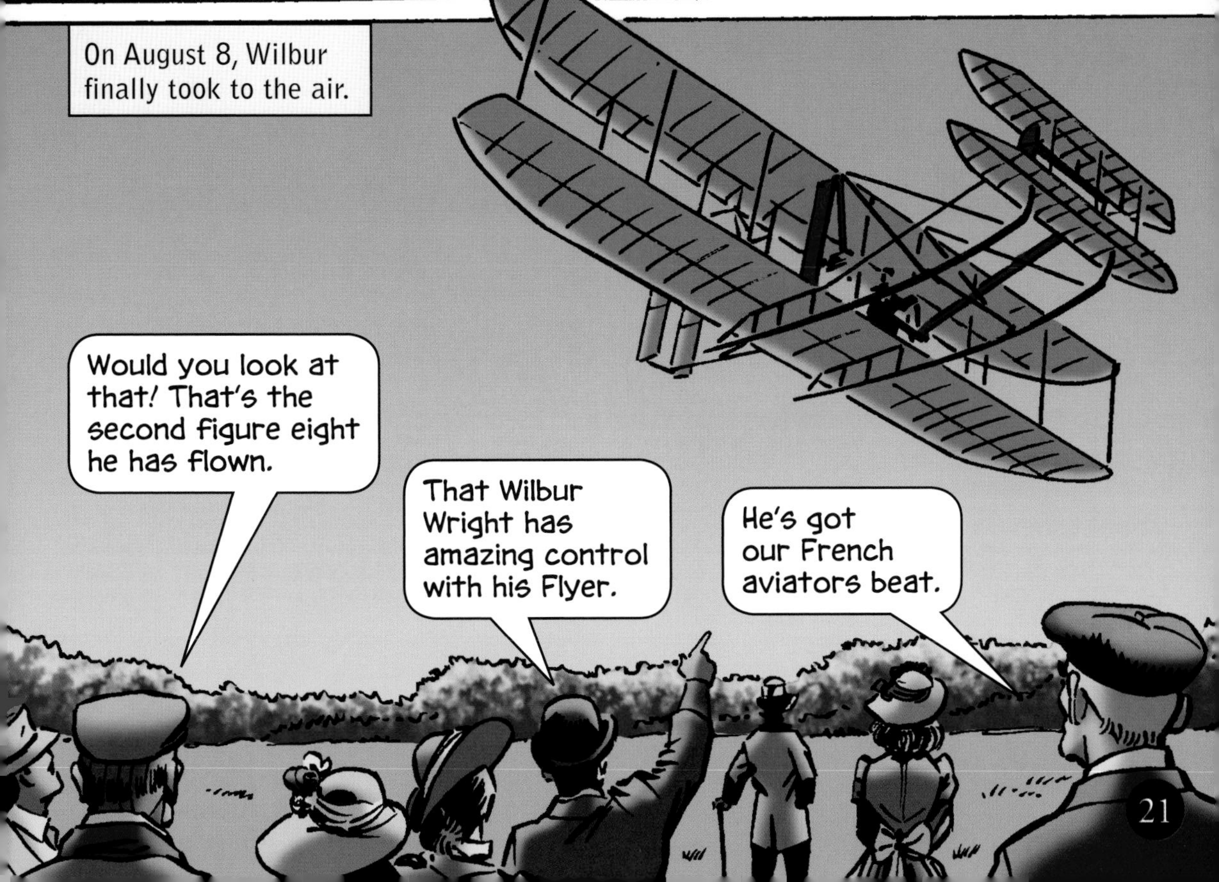
On August 8, Wilbur finally took to the air.
Would you look at that! That's the second figure eight he has flown.
That Wilbur Wright has amazing control with his Flyer.
He's got our French aviators beat.

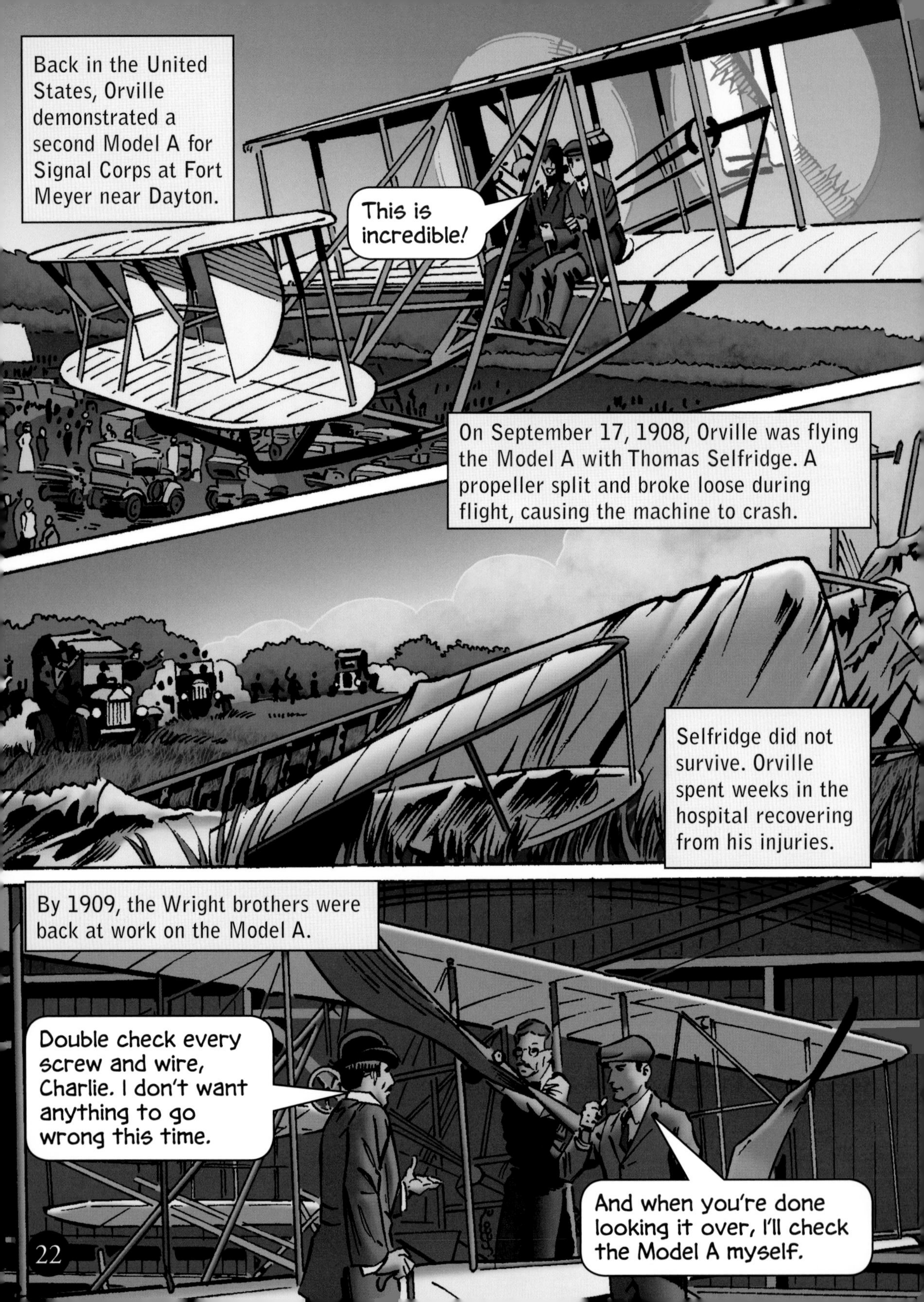
Back in the United States, Orville demonstrated a second Model A for Signal Corps at Fort Meyer near Dayton.
This is incredible!
On September 17, 1908, Orville was flying the Model A with Thomas Selfridge. A propeller split and broke loose during flight, causing the machine to crash.
Selfridge did not survive. Orville spent weeks in the hospital recovering from his injuries.
By 1909, the Wright brothers were back at work on the Model A.
Double check every screw and wire, Charlie. I don't want anything to go wrong this time.
And when you're done looking it over, I'll check the Model A myself.

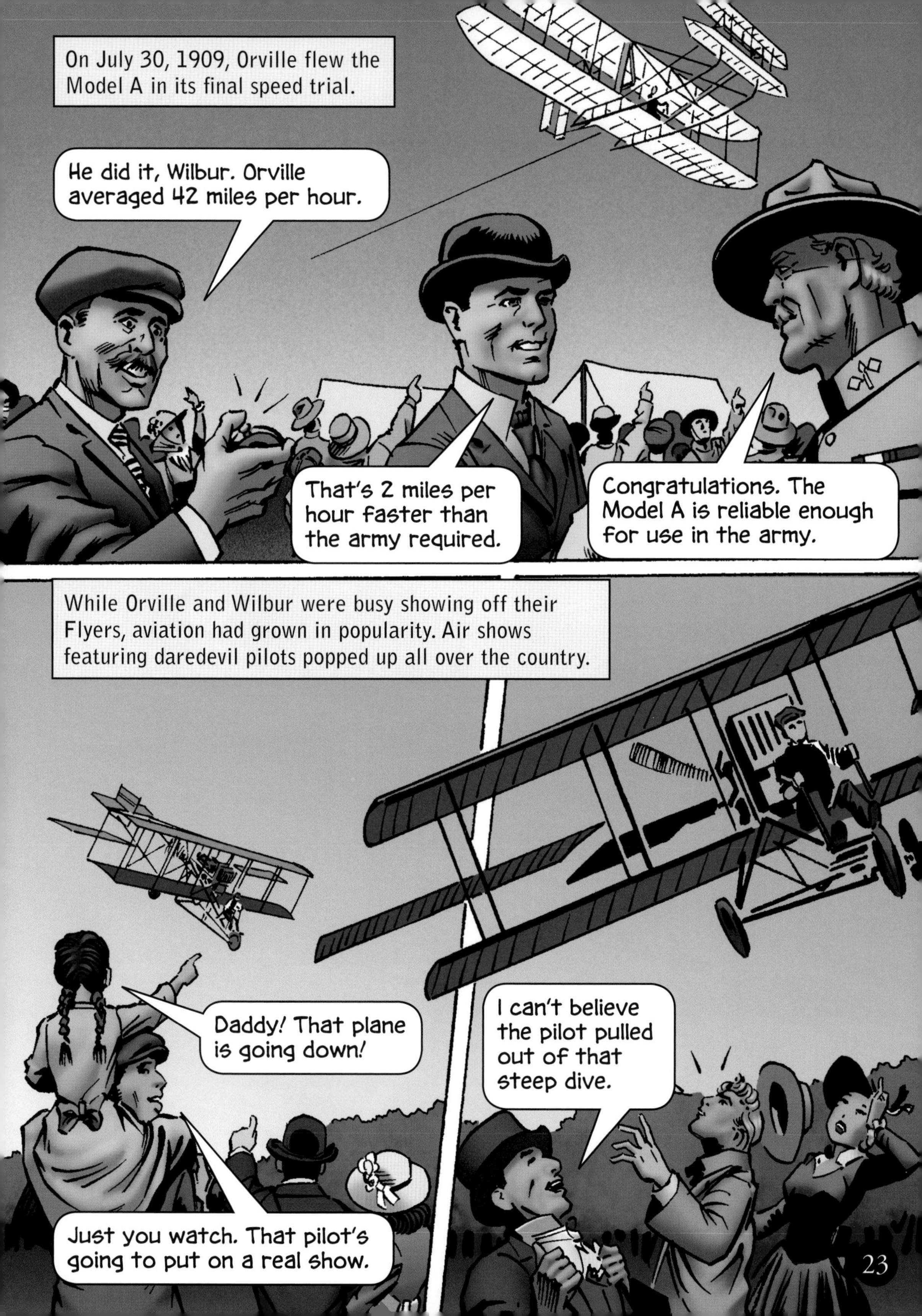

On July 30, 1909, Orville flew the Model A in its final speed trial.
He did it, Wilbur. Orville averaged 42 miles per hour.
That's 2 miles per hour faster than the army required.
Congratulations. The Model A is reliable enough for use in the army.
While Orville and Wilbur were busy showing off their Flyers, aviation had grown in popularity. Air shows featuring daredevil pilots popped up all over the country.
Daddy! That plane is going down!
Just you watch. That pilot's going to put on a real show.
I can't believe the pilot pulled out of that steep dive.

CHAPTER 4

AVIATION TAKES OFF

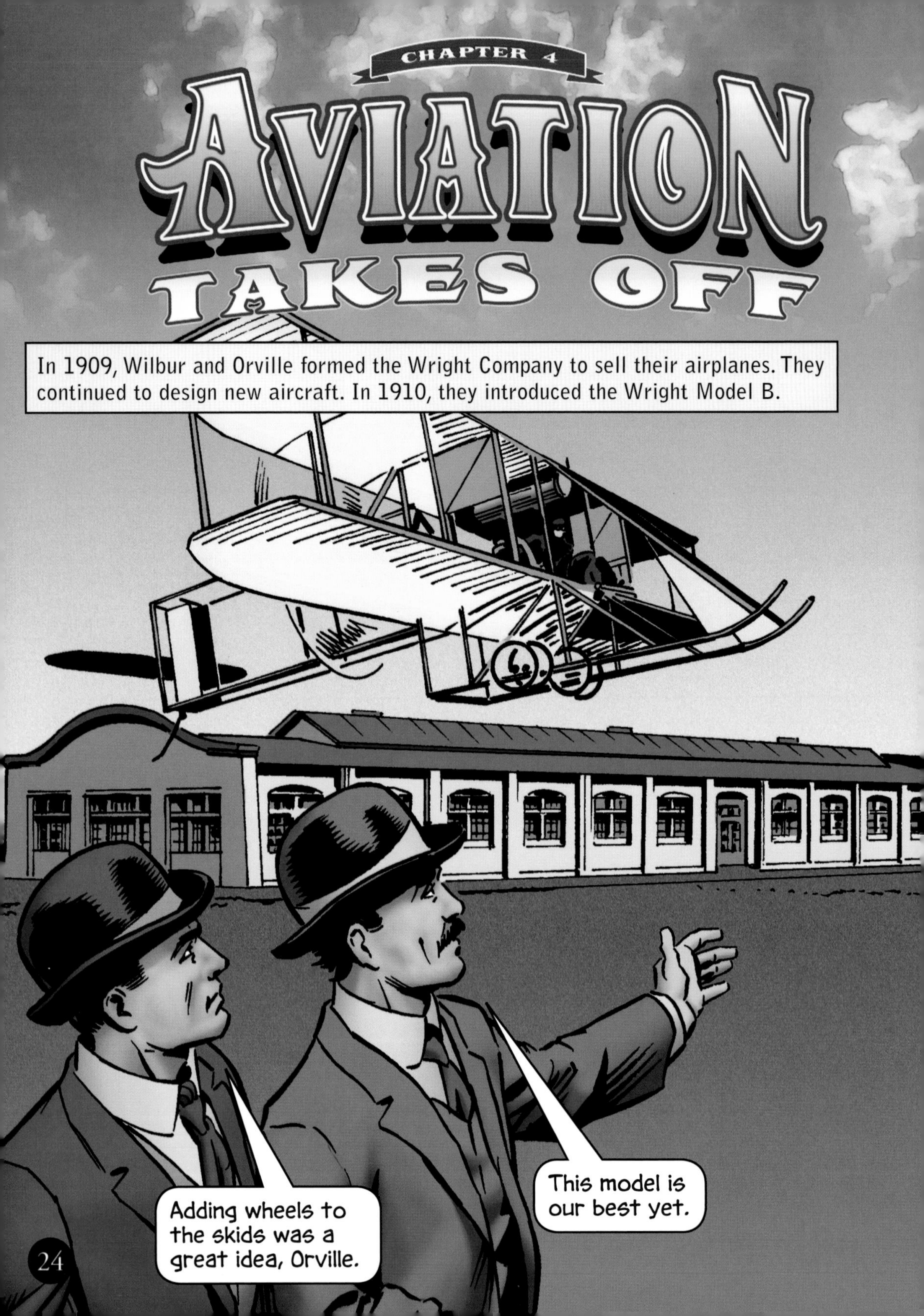
In 1909, Wilbur and Orville formed the Wright Company to sell their airplanes. They continued to design new aircraft. In 1910, they introduced the Wright Model B.
Adding wheels to the skids was a great idea, Orville.
This model is our best yet.

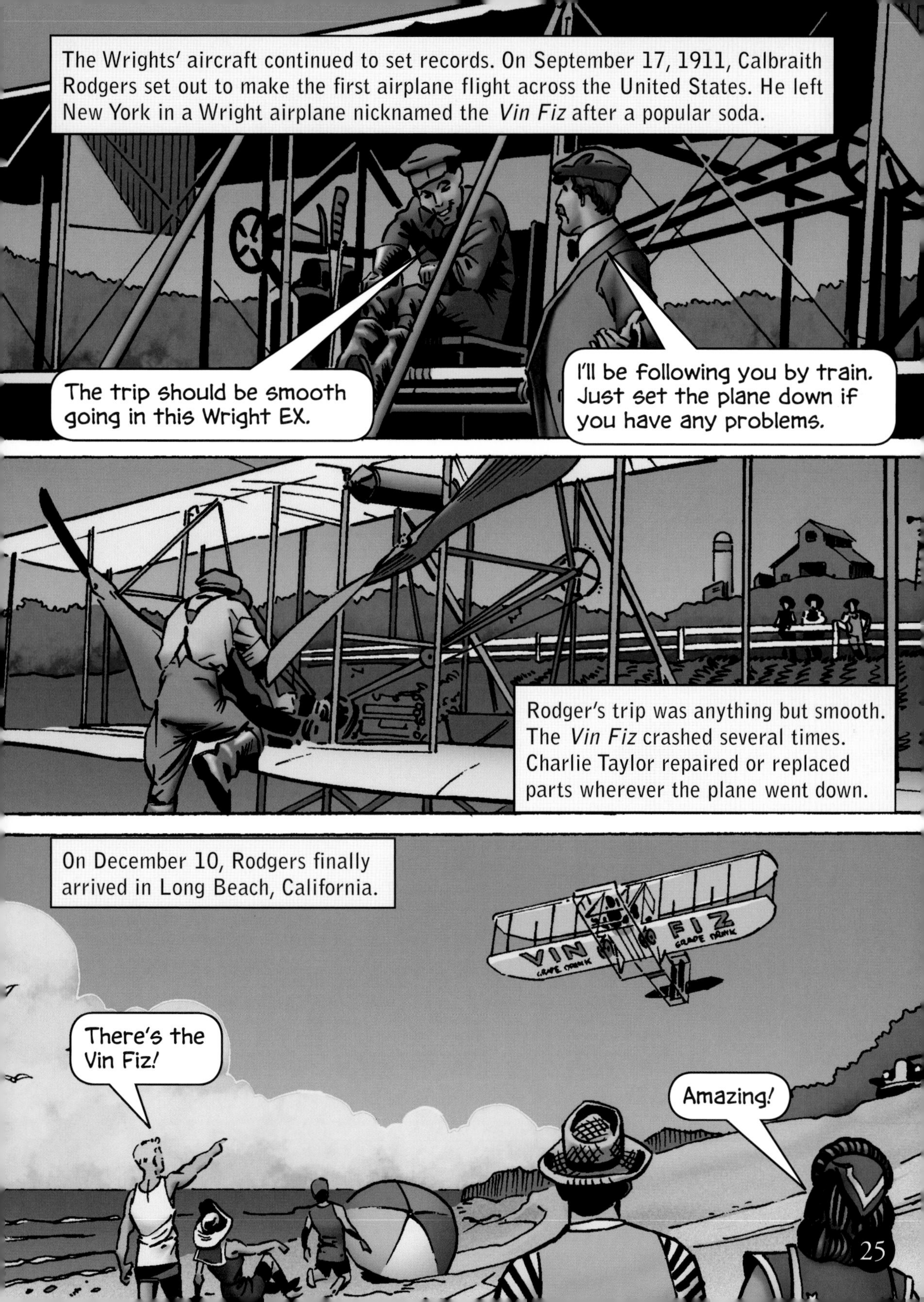
The Wrights' aircraft continued to set records. On September 17, 1911, Calbraith Rodgers set out to make the first airplane flight across the United States. He left New York in a Wright airplane nicknamed the *Vin Fiz* after a popular soda.
The trip should be smooth going in this Wright EX.
I'll be following you by train. Just set the plane down if you have any problems.
Rodger's trip was anything but smooth. The *Vin Fiz* crashed several times. Charlie Taylor repaired or replaced parts wherever the plane went down.
On December 10, Rodgers finally arrived in Long Beach, California.
VIN FIZ
GRAPE DRINK
There's the Vin Fiz!
Amazing!

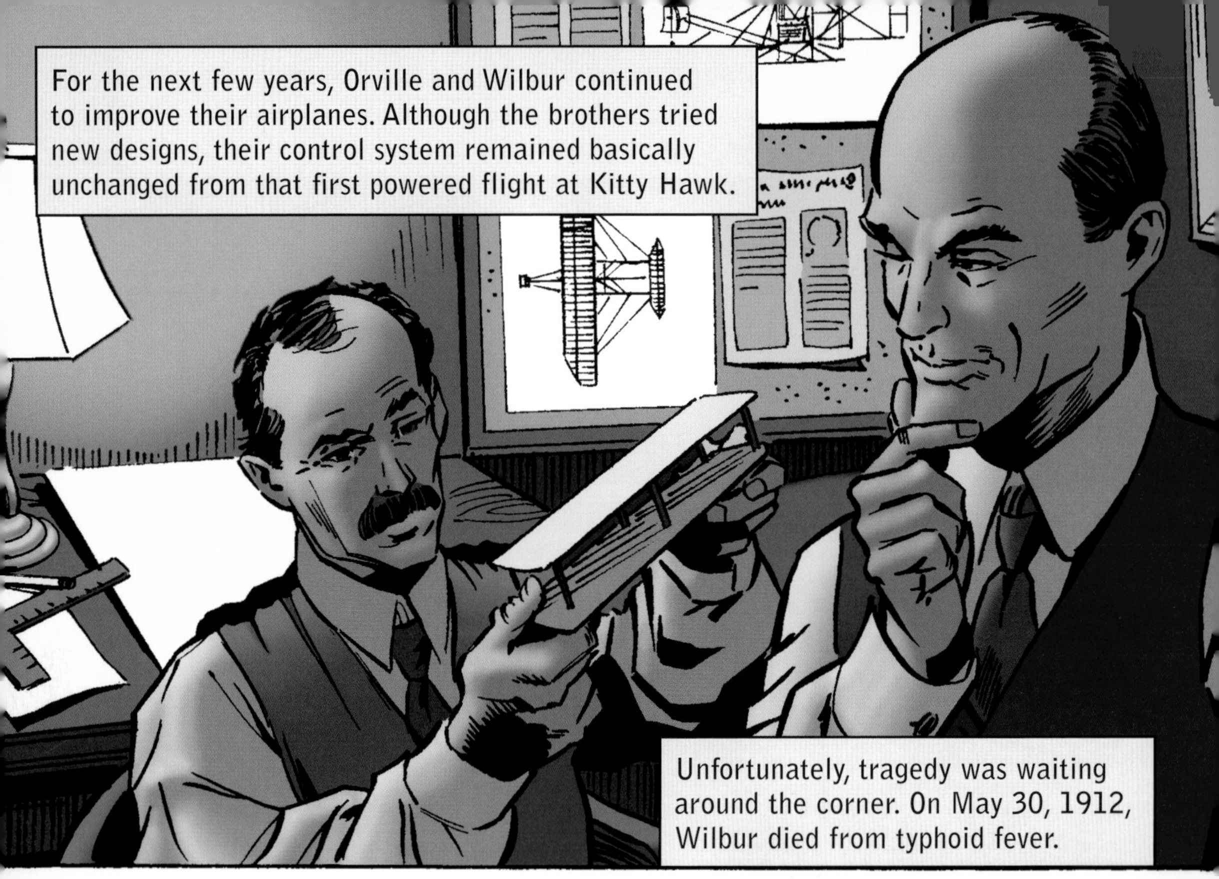
For the next few years, Orville and Wilbur continued to improve their airplanes. Although the brothers tried new designs, their control system remained basically unchanged from that first powered flight at Kitty Hawk.
Unfortunately, tragedy was waiting around the corner. On May 30, 1912, Wilbur died from typhoid fever.

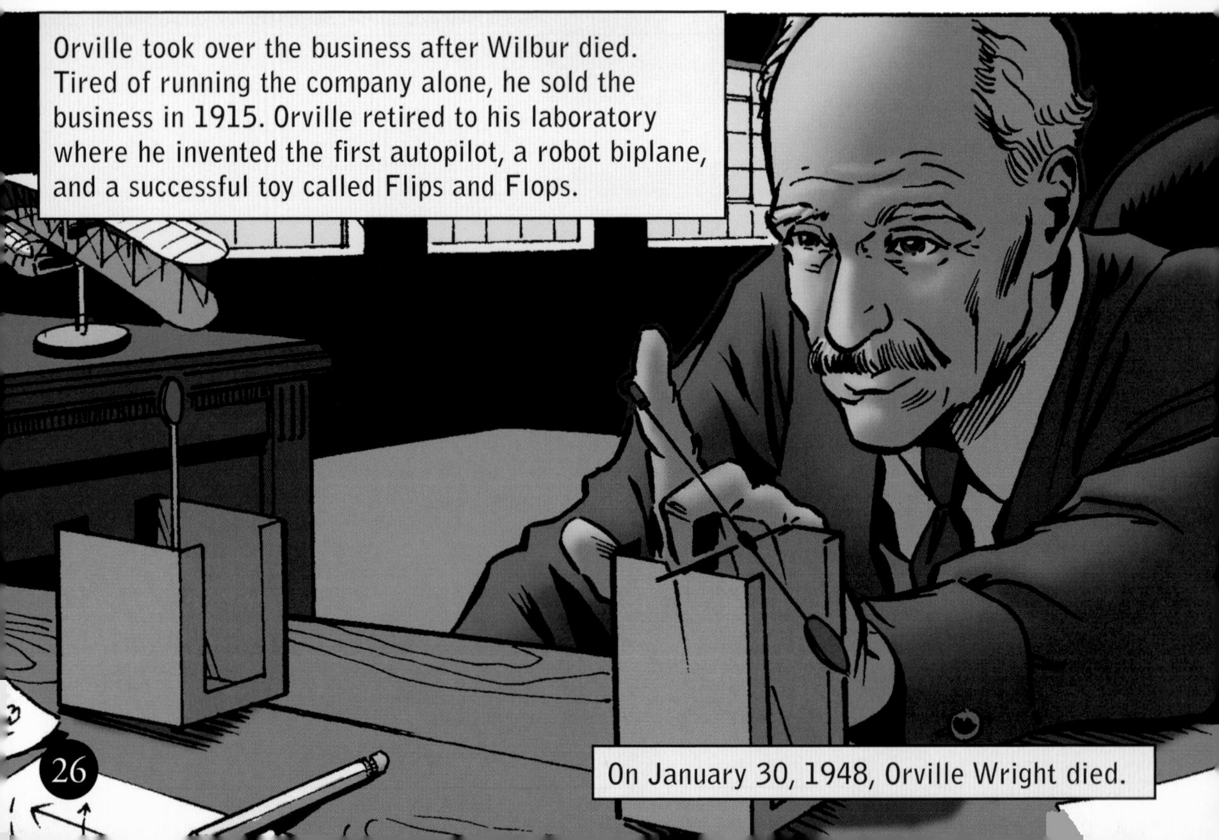
Orville took over the business after Wilbur died. Tired of running the company alone, he sold the business in 1915. Orville retired to his laboratory where he invented the first autopilot, a robot biplane, and a successful toy called Flips and Flops.
On January 30, 1948, Orville Wright died.

Today, airplanes carry people, food, and packages almost anywhere on earth.

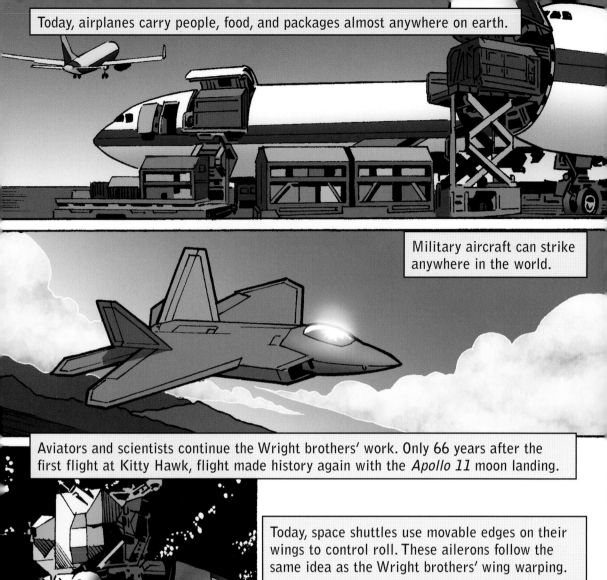

Military aircraft can strike anywhere in the world.

Aviators and scientists continue the Wright brothers' work. Only 66 years after the first flight at Kitty Hawk, flight made history again with the *Apollo 11* moon landing.

Today, space shuttles use movable edges on their wings to control roll. These ailerons follow the same idea as the Wright brothers' wing warping.

NASA
United States

USA

MORE ABOUT THE WRIGHT BROTHERS AND THE AIRPLANE

Wilbur Wright was born April 16, 1867, near Millville, Indiana. He died May 30, 1912, in Dayton, Ohio.

Orville Wright was born August 19, 1871, in Dayton, Ohio. He died January 30, 1948, after suffering a heart attack in his laboratory in Dayton.

One of the earliest inventors to study flight was Leonardo Da Vinci. In 1490, he made several attempts to design a flying machine, including a screwlike propeller that was an early model of the helicopter.

During their trips to Kitty Hawk, the brothers struggled with the wind, cold, sand, and bugs that swept across the dunes. At first, they camped in a small tent. Later, Orville and Wilbur built a small shed where they lived, and a hangar for their gliders and the Flyer.

Members of the U.S. Lifesaving Station at Kill Devil Hills helped the Wright brothers with takeoffs and landings. When Orville and Wilbur were ready to test their gliders and Flyers, they tacked a red flag to the side of the hangar. When crew members saw the flag, they headed to the dunes to help with the aircraft.

- The Wright brothers flew their 1902 glider at least 1,000 times off the sand dunes at Kitty Hawk. This glider set all the world records for gliding at that time, including one glide that went 622.5 feet in just 21 seconds. After the success of their 1902 glider, the Wright brothers were ready to build their powered machine.

- Some aviators claimed that they, not the Wright brothers, invented the airplane. In 1914, aircraft manufacturer Glenn Curtiss rebuilt and flew a version of the Great Aerodrome. This aircraft was invented by Samuel Langley in 1903. Langley had little success flying the large craft. Curtiss was able to fly the Aerodrome only after making several changes to Langley's design. Despite the changes, officials at the Smithsonian Institution declared that Langley invented the airplane. Orville fought this claim until 1942, when Smithsonian officials admitted that the Wright brothers were the airplane's true inventors. Today, millions of people view the first Wright Flyer at the Smithsonian.

- When *Apollo 11* astronaut Neil Armstrong walked on the moon, he paid tribute to the Wright brothers. In Armstrong's pocket was a piece of fabric from the Wright brothers' 1903 Flyer.

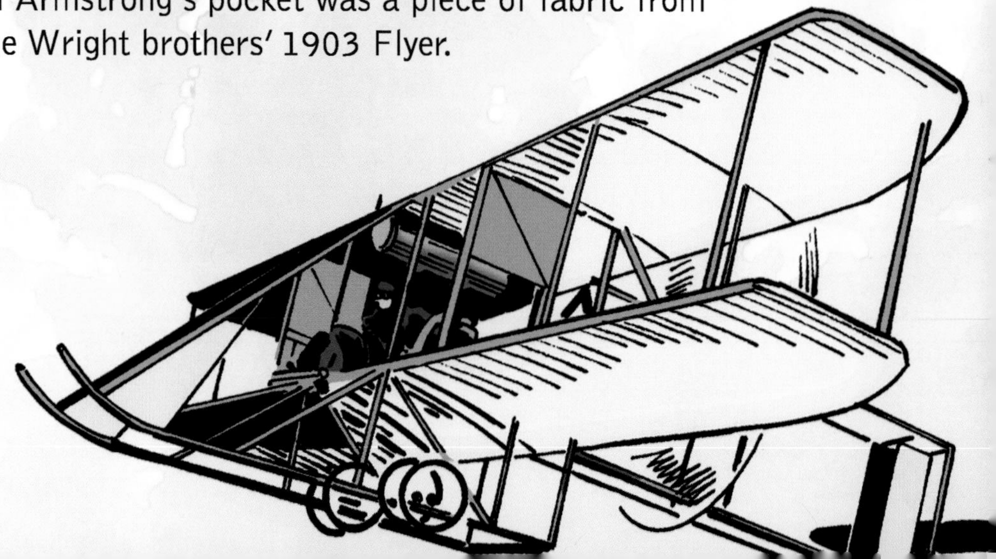

GLOSSARY

bank (BANGK)—to tilt an airplane sideways when turning

horsepower (HORSS-pou-ur)—a unit for measuring an engine's power

lift (LIFT)—the force that lets an airplane rise from the ground and stay in the air

patent (PAT-uhnt)—a legal document that gives an inventor the right to make, use, or sell an invention for a set period of years

pitch (PICH)—the angle of the blades on an aircraft; pitch determines whether an aircraft moves up or down.

roll (ROHL)—the movement of an airplane from side to side

skeptical (SKEP-tuh-kuhl)—to doubt that something is true

yaw (YAW)—the movement of an aircraft's nose from side to side

INTERNET SITES

FactHound offers a safe, fun way to find Internet sites related to this book. All of the sites on FactHound have been researched by our staff.

Here's how:
1. Visit *www.facthound.com*
2. Choose your grade level.
3. Type in this book ID **0736868453** for age-appropriate sites. You may also browse subjects by clicking on letters, or by clicking on pictures and words.
4. Click on the **Fetch It** button.

FactHound will fetch the best sites for you!

READ MORE

Hill, Lee Sullivan. *The Flyer Flew!: The Invention of the Airplane.* On My Own Science. Minneapolis: Millbrook Press, 2006.

Lynch, Emma. *The Wright Brothers.* Lives and Times. Chicago: Heinemann, 2005.

Masters, Nancy Robinson. *The Airplane.* Inventions that Shaped the World. New York: Franklin Watts, 2004.

Orr, Tamra. *The Dawn of Aviation: The Story of the Wright Brothers.* Monumental Milestones. Hockessin, Del.: Mitchell Lane, 2005.

BIBLIOGRAPHY

Crouch, Tom D. *The Bishop's Boys: A Life of Wilbur and Orville Wright.* New York: W. W. Norton, 1989.

Kelly, Fred C. *The Wright Brothers: A Biography Authorized by Orville Wright.* New York: Harcourt, Brace, and Company, 1943.

National Park Service: The Wright Brothers National Memorial (http://www.nps.gov/wrbr/).

Wright, Orville. *How We Invented the Airplane: An Illustrated History.* New York: Dover, 1988.

INDEX